W9-CSL-678

I LEARNED
KUNG FU
FROM A BEAR CUB

True Tales to make you Laugh, Chortle, Snicker and Feel Inspired

For Garry, Happy Travels! Matt Jackson

Edited by Matt Jackson
Summit Studios

Copyright © 2008 by Summit Studios. All rights reserved.
Introduction copyright © 2008 by Matthew Jackson

The use of any part of this publication reproduced, transmitted in any form or by any means, electronic, mechanical, photocopying, recording, or otherwise, or stored in a retrieval system, without the prior written consent of the publisher—or, in case of photocopying or other reprographic copying, a license from the Canadian Copyright Licensing Agency—is an infringement of copyright law.

Library and Archives Canada Cataloguing in Publication

I learned kung fu from a bear cub : true tales to make you laugh, chortle, snicker and feel inspired / edited by Matt Jackson.

ISBN 978-0-9734671-5-4
    1. Outdoor life--Canada--Humor. I. Jackson, Matt
PN6178.C3L423 2008   796.5'0971   C2008-903314-0

Designed by Kirk Seton, Signet Design Inc.
Cover Photo by Ron Niebrugge
Printed and bound in Canada

SUMMIT STUDIOS
#105, 2572 Birch St.
Vancouver, British Columbia
V6H 2T4 Canada

This book is dedicated to all travelers who venture forth bravely and come home with stories to share

Table of Contents

Introduction

By Matt Jackson

Like many teenagers, I traveled west as a young man, following the promise of opportunity and discovery to Canada's Banff National Park. I was a nineteen-year-old business student who had just finished his first year of university, and I was young, free from parental folds, and pining for a break from routine.

After more than three thousand kilometers behind the wheel, my friend Jason and I arrived in the small mountain village of Lake Louise, where we planned to spend the summer working. It didn't take me long to find a job stocking shelves at a small grocery store, which was a welcome change from academia. My apartment was surrounded by peaks and glaciers; wilderness trails began two minutes from my back door; and I occasionally caught glimpses of woodland critters that were our nearby neighbors. I was enthralled. Never before had I lived in such close proximity to nature.

Not long after I arrived in Lake Louise, I heard a story underlining just how thin this barrier separating civilization from nature can be. A bear, looking for some quick take-out, wandered out of the forest one morning and climbed through the open window of a parked transport truck not far from my residence. Awakened by rustling noises, the groggy truck driver peeled back the curtain from his sleeping berth to find the inquisitive bruin seated behind the truck's steering wheel, chugging the remainder of a two-liter carton of chocolate milk.

Later, that same bear became fascinated by the automatic sliding-glass doors at a local hotel. Whenever the bear stepped forward, the doors opened; whenever he stepped back, the doors closed. The concierge had a bit of a fright when the bruin—presumably wanting a dinner reservation—wandered into the lobby. Their brochure had advertised wildlife viewing, but most guests presumed the critters would stay *outside* the hotel.

There's something about encounters with wild animals that people adore. The North American tourism industry generates tens of billions of dollars annually on fish and wildlife-related recreation; we also insist that our governments protect wildlife through legislation, which they do to some extent. And few people who've had a close encounter with a whale, a bear, or a moose don't love the chance to share their story with fellow travelers. These chance sightings often become the highlights of a trip. The journey is the cake; wildlife encounters are the sweetest, most delectable of icings.

After publishing our first anthology, *Mugged by a Moose*, we received a lot of enthusiastic feedback relating to the stories about human–moose encounters. And for that reason, we've now decided to dig up and publish a few of the wackiest stories we've heard about encounters with bears—those furry, rotund, charismatic (and potentially dangerous) monarchs of the North American wilderness.

One of the most intriguing things about bears is their ability, at times, to take on human characteristics. They are intelligent animals with unique personalities, which is probably why wildlife officials use the word "unpredictable" when describing how a wild bear will react after encountering a human. They'll probably run in the other direction—but it's also possible they could bluff-charge, or worse yet, attack you. Or, in the case of down-on-your-luck bruins from the West Coast, they might simply hold out a tin can and ask for your spare change. You just never know.

In the case of Carolyn Kohler and her husband Tom—veteran, bear-aware outdoors people from northern California—they finally met their match while camping amidst the sapphire-tinged lakes of the Ansel Adams Wilderness. The scavenging bear they met was as persistent and ingenious as they come in his efforts to liberate their bag of food. Another bear—one that Ontario fishing guide Marty Descoteaux happened upon while trolling with his downrigger on Esten Lake—set his sights on a much bigger prize: the unsuspecting guide's fishing boat.

As we've done with our previous titles, of course, we've tried to include a variety of themes, styles, and subjects in these books. You'll find much more in these pages than just bear stories. There are plenty of other tales to get you laughing, like Robert Fulton's irresistible description of his attempts to take pictures of a waterfall with his new ProPhotographer Signature Model tripod. Or the unbelievable tale of how Wayne Van Sickle managed to accidentally send a friend to Anchorage, Alaska without his wallet, identification, toothbrush, or … his pants.

You'll also find a few stories about North Americans traveling abroad. It's hard not to appreciate the effort Jeremy Kroeker makes to impress a lovely female colleague at a Swiss mountaineering school—especially when you see how horribly wrong that goes. Or the marathon of mishaps Philip Blazdell endures on a Land Rover safari to the Ngorongoro Conservation Area in Tanzania.

There are even a few stories that might best be described as contemplative. My favorite is "Kojo's Island" by Chris Czajkowski, which tells the tale of how this longtime wilderness homesteader bonded with a Japanese volunteer named Jun at her remote wilderness cabin in north central British Columbia.

Like me, Jun set out as a young man in search of adventure, enticed by the promise of opportunity and discovery. He had grown up in Tokyo, so he was even less prepared for the rigors of living in the wilderness than I would have been at his age. At Chris's cabin, drinking water had to be hauled from the lake and boiled; firewood had to be chopped to cook dinner; and calls of nature were answered in the outhouse.

Jun hadn't anticipated living in such close proximity to wild animals, either. One day, while doing some trail maintenance work a few kilometers from the main cabin, the young man from Tokyo encountered a bear. Not knowing what to do, he nervously retreated to a nearby canoe, smoked two cigarettes, then returned to his post and began working again. To warn the bear of his presence, he started singing loudly in his native Japanese.

It was only later that evening, after Jun had told Chris about his brush with danger, that she was able to set him straight.

"Singing in Japanese is no good," she told him. "It's a Canadian bear. It can only understand English."

Travel Insurance

When boldness leads to a large hospital bill.

By Jeremy Kroeker

I had never even considered buying travel insurance until confronted by the horrified expression of a travel agent named Gwen. Having grown up in Saskatchewan, the province that *invented* free health care in Canada, I felt entitled to a universal "Get Out of Hospital Free" card. Besides, I had youth, health, and dumb luck on my side. What could possibly happen to me at a mountaineering school in such a civilized country as Austria?

Gwen's worried expression made me reconsider. Perhaps a few extra dollars spent would reduce the stress of my first intercontinental journey, at least for Gwen. When I agreed to buy the insurance, she slumped back in her chair and let out a sigh of relief. I completed the paperwork, and she shook my hand and wished me a safe journey.

But seriously, what could happen to me in Austria?

A few days later my train deposited me at the station in Schladming, a quaint village nestled in the hazy blue Austrian Alps. The town comprised cobblestone roads, wooden bridges, clock towers, and orderly shops. It also laid claim to Tauernhof, the mountaineering school I had come to attend.

The school mainly attracted North American boys like myself. In our minds, we would spend the days frolicking with golden-haired Austrian maidens in alpine meadows under the soft caress of the summer sun.

Unfortunately, the director viewed the school's curriculum in a slightly different light. Following an ambiguous orientation and several boring icebreaker games, we relinquished our watches to the powers that be and stumbled into the mountains under the cover of early morning darkness. Ulli, our lanky German guide, had shaggy black hair and a beard that looked as if it might try to escape. He never quite found pants capable of concealing his ankles, nor the correct English phrase for any idea he wished to express. Nevertheless, his quiet, gentle nature made him a pleasant companion.

Our little band of intrepid adventurers whiled away many wonderful days in the Austrian Alps, climbing, caving, and hiking under Ulli's watchful eye. Against all odds, a seed of romance sprouted between myself and a beautiful girl from Ontario. I couldn't believe my good fortune. Yes, I had reached a pinnacle in my young life and it seemed as though things could not possibly get better.

Pinnacles can be precarious, of course. I learned that lesson while hiking through an alpine meadow alive with wildflowers and velvet grass. That was where our group came upon a lethargic little snake sunning itself on the path.

The animal reminded me of the common garter snakes found on the Canadian prairies—harmless, really. It looked like the kind of snake little boys capture to torment little girls with on a lazy summer day. I suddenly had a brilliant idea: I would seize the serpent and impress the Ontario girl with my bravery.

Long before Ulli could articulate an objection in English, I stumbled forward and grabbed the snake behind its head. From my limited experience with garter snakes, I knew that if I caught the animal just so, it would be unable to turn and strike. Then again, garter snakes seldom bite, even when handled improperly. This little monster, in contrast, demonstrated agility and aggression far superior to any garter snake I had ever handled improperly. It unleashed a blood-chilling hiss and, with the practiced precision of a trained predator, spun its head completely around and pierced my left thumb with a fang that seemed improbably long for such a small creature.

I caught the snake to impress a girl. Mission accomplished. My new goal—detaching myself from the hissing snake that dangled from my thumb by a single fang—proved more difficult. I held the reptile at shoulder height with an outstretched arm and considered my options.

I momentarily thought about grabbing it by the tail and ripping it out of my flesh, but that seemed unwise. The only alternative— and the one I chose—was panic, which came more naturally. I hopped around, gesticulating wildly with my arms and screaming like an eight-year-old boy playing kissing tag at recess. The snake eventually dropped to the ground and slithered away, shaken but unharmed.

Ulli followed me for the rest of the afternoon, nervously breaking the silence every few minutes to ask how I felt. Mostly, I felt embarrassed. But my thumb had also swollen considerably, turned purple, and begun throbbing with a dull pain. As we walked, the pain crept into my hand, then my elbow, then my shoulder.

When the venom eventually reached its icy fingers into my neck and jaw, Ulli said, "This isn't funny any more," implying that he had considered my pain amusing until that moment. He radioed for Hans Peter, the director, who arrived remarkably quickly, as though carried by the wind.

Hans Peter was a wiry Austrian mountaineer with blond hair and piercing blue eyes. He spoke softly, but with intimidating authority, conveying a certain quiet assurance that his masculinity was beyond reproach. Like most Austrian men, he could manage to look tough while wearing an outfit that included tight leather shorts with suspenders, wool socks hiked up to the knees, and a frilly pastel shirt with embroidered flowers. He had the air of a father figure about him; it made you want to seek his approval. I'll never forget his first words to me.

"Jeremy, you idiot."

"That's just what my mom used to say," I stammered.

"What were you thinking?" he continued.

Now, a guy like me gets asked that question a lot over the course of his life. I have never really answered it to anyone's complete satisfaction. Honesty is seldom the right tack, and the same goes for humor, though I briefly considered saying, "I collect venom." In the end I said nothing, which was undoubtedly the correct response.

Hans Peter marched me away from Ulli and my friends, some of whom wished me a melodramatic and final farewell. After a few minutes of hurried hiking we found a tiny alpine hut inhabited by two sturdy elderly women. Hans Peter explained the situation to them—undoubtedly emphasizing that I was an idiot—and the women sprung into action, clucking their tongues and worriedly shaking their heads.

One woman poured me a glass of warm milk and the other spread a clean blanket over her bed, motioning for me to lie down. Then they turned to leave. Before Hans Peter shut the door, he turned to me and said in the most impressively callous manner, "People have been killed by snakes in this region. You might die."

With that he closed the door, leaving me alone with that very cheery thought.

I lay in a one-room shack with a small entryway and adjoining pantry. The shack, built from weathered, rough-hewn timber, had no decorations except a bouquet of wildflowers on the wooden table and a lacy white curtain drawn over the room's only window. I tried to rest and wondered if some of the last words I would ever hear would be, "Jeremy, you idiot. You might die."

I thought about dying. I had always put on a brave face when the subject came up in conversation, but I had never before confronted the *actual* possibility of death. I tried to relax and pray, but not for healing—just that my mom would find comfort if I did die. As it turned out, I felt prepared to cross that river, shuffle off this mortal coil, kick the bucket, buy the farm ... but I digress.

After immeasurable moments of self-reflection (immeasurable because Hans Peter still had my watch) it occurred to me that I had no idea what would happen next. Hans Peter had been somewhat vague regarding the details. Then I heard the deep thumping of a helicopter's rotors beating the air somewhere in the distance. The thumping grew louder as the helicopter drew near, laboring for purchase in the thin mountain air. I stepped outside to watch a cumbersome military machine set down in the meadow, as if the pilot were loath to crush any wildflowers. I boarded the machine and waved to Hans Peter as we lifted off; to my great relief, he smiled and waved back.

Though the flight to Shladming lasted a mere four minutes, I had a lot of time to think. It occurred to me that my grasp of the German language might prove inadequate when faced with a medical emergency. Eager to amuse myself and confuse the locals, the very first thing I'd learned to say in German was, "I am a pretty village." I'd quickly added other expressions to my useless German arsenal, such as, "You are a platypus" and "I have a bunion." Unfortunately, my linguistic prowess had not significantly improved since my arrival in Austria.

The helicopter touched down, depositing me at the hospital's emergency ward. Doctors and nurses rallied around me, shouting at each other in German (the words "platypus" and "bunion" were conspicuously absent). They rushed me to a sterile room with bright lights and placed me on a metal table. A doctor shouted orders to the medical team and then hurried out of the room, his stethoscope swinging wildly about his neck.

The hospital staff's high level of emotion and activity eventually became unsustainable. The room quieted down and my crack medical team shuffled off without having really done anything. Seizing this opportunity, a male nurse unsheathed the single largest needle I have ever seen in my life and prepared to deliver a mighty blow to my now-bare backside. Years later, I can still see the nurse backing up several paces to get a run at me, standing with needle in hand and windmilling his arm for dramatic effect. But that might be a slight distortion of my memory.

More to the point, the fact that the nurse appeared to be acting alone on this decision did give me some measure of discomfort. I briefly considered calling for help, but all I could have shouted was, "I am a pretty village!"

Fortunately, at the last possible moment a doctor returned; he shouted angrily at the nurse and snatched the syringe from his hand.

For three days I lay in the hospital, unable to communicate with patients or staff because of the language barrier. I sought solace in the pages of an English Bible and committed to memory Jeremiah 8:17, which reads, "'See, I will send venomous snakes among you, vipers that cannot be charmed, and they will bite you,' declares the Lord."

At the end of my solitary confinement, Ulli came to pick me up at the hospital. The pain in my arm remained, and would linger for another month. Although I never received any actual treatment, the hospital bill came to two thousand Canadian dollars … billed to and paid for by my travel insurance company. (I imagine that my picture still hangs above every executive toilet in their corporate head office.)

Ulli smiled as we climbed into his car and said, "I'm glad to see you're all right. Now Hans Peter has another story to tell."

My travel agent, Gwen, also likes to tell the story. She sells way more travel insurance than she used to.

Despite living in oil-rich Calgary, Alberta, Jeremy Kroeker prefers the financially "unburdened" life of being a travel writer. His first book, Motorcycle Therapy, *is about a three-month motorcycle journey from Calgary to Panama. He's currently working on a second book about a motorcycle trip through the Middle East and North Africa. Follow his continuing adventures at* ***www.JeremyKroeker.com***.

To Alaska (Without Pants)

A place where pants and passports are clearly optional.

By Wayne Van Sickle

When I was twenty-four years old, I lived in Southern Ontario and drove a Jeep. No matter where I took that Jeep, it felt either underutilized or unwelcome. Once, I decided to drive over a curb and onto a hilly, unkempt, abandoned field that was dotted with trees. When I came back out to the road thirty minutes later, a police car was waiting for me. The land was private property and I was warned never to come back.

That's when I decided to go to Alaska.

I was young and more than a bit naïve, but somehow I managed to convince my good friend Josh and my cousin Barb to come with me. We sketched out a basic plan for a three-month summer road trip. There were countless things we wanted to see and do in the Land of the Midnight Sun: among them were to see a grizzly bear, climb a mountain, visit Denali National Park, and hike the Chilkoot Trail. We planned to drive west and start with a month-long exploration of the Alaska Panhandle. Afterwards, we would spend another two months exploring Alaska's spacious interior.

Five days before departure date in May, my cousin Barb fell down a flight of stairs and broke her leg. Not surprisingly, she had to cancel. Josh and I were saddened and disappointed, and we were also worried about how we were going to pay for gas money. After all, Alaska is a long way from southern Ontario, and as students of the University of Waterloo, Josh and I were living on Student Budgets. It looked like we might have to cancel the trip, so we invited everyone we could think of to join us. Nobody was available at such short notice.

And so, less than three days before our scheduled departure, Josh and I turned to the patrons of a well-known Uptown Waterloo establishment—the Heuther Hotel—for help.

I am not sure if there is actually a hotel at the Heuther, but there is certainly a brewery. They make their own beer and serve it in a wonderful old stone basement pub. It took two nights of canvassing pub-goers to find someone with a flexible summer schedule, the desire to go north, and the financial means to do it. His name was Jason, a friend of a friend.

Jason didn't profess to know much about outdoor pursuits, but he sure could get a lot done in a short amount of time. In a span of two days he negotiated a leave of absence from the cookie company where he worked, sold his motorcycle to finance to the trip, drove his girlfriend to the airport for a flight to Austria (where she was spending the summer), and bought everything we told him he would need for camping. We pulled out of town right on schedule: me, Josh, and our new friend Jason. We didn't even know our new travel companion's last name, and we didn't learn it for two days because he slept for the first 2,600 kilometers as we drove west.

Alaska bills itself as "the Last Frontier." It's a place where the sun doesn't rise in the dead of winter, and where it doesn't set in the height of summer. It attracts more than its fair share of strangeness. Looking back, we should have known that someone would end up in Anchorage without pants.

Despite our trip's inauspicious start, we pulled into Prince Rupert, BC on time to catch the overnight ferry to Ketchikan, Alaska. Our Lonely Planet guidebook told us that the geography of the Alaska Panhandle is so rugged that there are no roads between its principal communities of Ketchikan, Wrangell, St. Petersburg, and Juneau, which are connected by a system of state ferries called the Alaska Marine Highway. The ferries are equipped with cabins that passengers can rent for the night, but savvy travelers like us (i.e., those without a lot of money) choose to pitch their tents on the upper deck. This probably makes the Alaska Marine Highway the *only* highway in North America that lets you set up your tent on top of the vehicle you are traveling on.

It's quiet in the middle of the night out on the waters of the Inside Passage. Mornings, however, can be somewhat less tranquil. The more outgoing captains of the ferries use their boats' public address systems to keep their passengers apprised of animal sightings. Unbeknownst to us, a loudspeaker was mounted to a post directly behind our tent, so on our first morning in Alaska, we were jolted awake by the piercing nasal pitch of the captain's voice shouting, "Humpback whale on the port side!"

This is exactly the way any young traveler wants to be wakened his first morning in Alaska. Josh ripped the tent's zipper open and we burst out running. Josh went left and I went right—having never served in the navy, neither one of us knew which direction "port" was.

Jason was less impulsive. He looked around to see which way most of the other passengers were going, and simply followed the crowd to the sighting.

We all met at the port side of the boat (port turned out to be the left) in time to see the whale. Few sights in the animal kingdom are as awesome as a fifty-foot, seventy-nine-thousand-pound humpback whale breaching. The whale swims to the surface at top speed and shoots into the air, then crashes back down again. That morning, our humpback must have breached more than twenty-five times just a few hundred yards from the ferry. We were in awe.

Alaska is a tough place, as we learned in Wrangell, a tiny settlement at the mouth of the Stikine River. A sign on the wall over the pool table in the local pub made us think twice before getting in any arguments with a local over a pool game. It read: *Think twice—if you break a pool cue it will cost you 35 dollars.*

A band was in town that night, and like everyone else in Wrangell we decided to take in the show. Right from the start we noticed a bit of tension among the band members. The tension grew throughout the evening and came to a head during the second set when the drummer threw down his sticks, walked out from behind his drum kit and punched the bass player squarely in the face, successfully breaking his nose. The guitarist and the singer didn't miss a beat; they kept playing as the bass player fell to his knees, blood dripping into his hands. The drummer climbed back behind his kit and joined in to the song again. No one in the crowd even seemed to notice as the bassist hobbled offstage.

Later, we learned that this band had been through Wrangell before and everyone knew that the bassist was unpopular with his bandmates due to his drinking problem; he had apparently caused much grief on previous tours. Apparently, he had promised not to drink on this latest outing, and to keep him honest, the rest of the band had made him sign a contract giving them permission to punch him in the face anytime he was caught having a drink.

Be careful if you ever visit Alaska: the rye and cokes really pack a punch!

The community of Skagway is the transition point between the Panhandle and the rest of Alaska. From Skagway, one can drive north to Whitehorse and from there, to Anchorage and beyond. This small town is also the place where many hikers like us pick up last-minute supplies for the Chilkoot Trail, which starts at nearby Dyea.

Hiking the Chilkoot Trail is by far the best history class I have ever taken. After gold was discovered in the Klondike in 1896, thousands of men from around the world came north to the Yukon with dreams of striking it rich. Most arrived in Skagway by boat because the shortest route into the Yukon Territory was to hike over the Chilkoot Pass along what became known as the Chilkoot Trail. The trail starts in Alaska and ends in Canada, where the bulk of the gold was found.

With thousands of desperate men showing up daily, the Mounties took action to prevent the rampant theft and general lawlessness that had been associated with all other gold rushes around the world. They controlled the flow of prospectors into Canada by setting up a border station at the top of the Chilkoot Pass, and they passed a law that required prospectors to bring with them two thousand pounds of goods and supplies—enough to function independently for an entire year.

Few prospectors could afford to pay for the services of porters, so most made many trips across the treacherous pass in the middle of winter. At the top, the prospectors handed their gear to the Mounties, who weighed it, catalogued it, and warehoused it. When a man had packed up all the required provisions, he was welcomed into Canada. The average man spent three months packing in his supplies.

In 1897, between twenty and thirty thousand prospectors crossed into Canada; once over the Chilkoot, most of them built a raft and floated down the Yukon River to the Klondike gold fields.

These days, the fifty-three-kilometer-long Chilkoot Trail is one of the premier treks in North America. It begins at sea level and passes through lush coastal rainforest on its rapid ascent to the Chilkoot's crown in the alpine. We started at the trailhead mid-morning, and although the first day offers mostly flat walking, the packs weighed heavily on our shoulders and hips. Our thoughts turned to methods of lightening the packs.

That night, snug in the day-use cabin at our designated campsite, we unpacked all our food and started consuming the heaviest items: fruit and liquor. As we stuffed our faces, we noticed a young guy about our age sitting alone with a bottle of Wild Turkey and four oranges. Apparently, he had come to the same conclusion we had reached. He looked like he needed assistance, so we went over and sat down.

Chad was a university student from Toledo, Ohio, and like us, he was spending the summer in Alaska. Chad worked at a backpacking store in his hometown. He had a keen sense of wit, and he had us laughing almost as soon as we met him. By the time we had helped him drain his bottle of Wild Turkey, we were fast friends and decided to hike the remainder of the trail together.

The trek was truly outstanding, five days of divine scenery that seemed to change around every bend. Along the trail were many rusting artifacts left behind by gold-hungry prospectors. The pass itself was steep and arduous, but exhilarating. As we approached the top of the pass, crossed it, and continued down and over the eye-popping alpine tundra beside a string of azure lakes, we felt as though we ourselves had passed through history. Happily, at the end, we learned that Chad was planning to go to Anchorage next, just like us. That afternoon we decided to drive north to Whitehorse, clean up, have a burger, and organize ourselves for Alaska.

With four guys, three mountain bikes, and all our camping gear, there was barely room to breathe in my Jeep. After the short drive to Whitehorse, it was clear we couldn't make the long drive to Anchorage like this. Fortunately, Chad had purchased an Alaska and Yukon bus pass, which gave him unlimited travel in the north. He wisely suggested that we make our separate ways to Anchorage, where we could meet up and resume our adventures together.

There was only one bus per week from Whitehorse to Anchorage, and Chad's bus schedule showed that it left the following morning at 10:30. We planned to party it up on the town that night and drop Chad at the bus station the next morning. Jason, Josh, and I had a few errands to run in the Whitehorse area before leaving for Anchorage, and we planned to see a few sights along the way, so we agreed to meet Chad at the Anchorage Youth Hostel in five days.

We set up our tents at the Robert Service Campground at the outskirts of Whitehorse before our night on the town commenced. We ended up at a bar called the Loose Moose, which had a dance floor and a drink special of tequila shooters for ninety-nine cents. Josh was allergic to tequila, but that didn't stop him. We lived it up that night, partying like there was no tomorrow, which meant that although we each made it back to the tent that night, no one thought to set the alarm.

I woke up with a pounding headache at 10:15. Slowly, and in barely perceptible degrees, it dawned on me that Chad's bus was scheduled to depart in fifteen minutes. And the bus station was on the other side of town!

I sprang into action, a Grade-A tequila migraine working its morning magic on my noggin as I shook Chad awake and scrambled out of our tent to start the Jeep. Chad staggered out and stared through his tequila-shooter-induced coma. From the driver's seat, I kicked open the passenger door and he flopped himself inside.

I'm certain I broke most of the Yukon Territory's traffic laws that morning, but I did make it to the bus station on time. I pulled up directly behind the Anchorage-bound bus as the driver wrestled luggage into the storage compartment underneath and passengers filed onto the bus. Chad stumbled out of the Jeep and I shoveled him into the middle of the line, which parted for his arrival. I waved as he disappeared up the stairs and into the Greyhound's maw. (Always one to pay attention to detail, I double-checked the destination board on the bus and confirmed that it was in fact the Anchorage bus.) Then I drove straight back to the campground, crawled into my tent, and eased back into my sleeping bag. I was asleep by the time my head hit the makeshift pillow of my fleece jacket.

Josh, Jason, and I woke up later that afternoon and went into Whitehorse for a late breakfast, then spent the rest of the day and early evening walking around Whitehorse, doing the tourist thing. I phoned my parents back home in Waterloo and learned that my Jeep had been recalled for servicing due to some sort of mechanical problem. Fortunately there was a dealership in Whitehorse, so I made an appointment. We had a quiet evening and went to sleep early that night.

The following morning we got up in good time and went about taking down the tent and packing up. Jason made breakfast while Josh emptied the tents, and I packed everything into the Jeep. After traveling together for a month, we knew who owned each piece of equipment and clothing—and that's why I was somewhat surprised when I heard Josh call out from the tent, "Hey guys, whose pants are these?"

They were not my pants, nor Jason's, which was initially quite puzzling. But the owner's identity became abundantly clear as Josh found other items he didn't recognize: a shaving kit, a pair of hiking boots, a backpack, a wallet full of American money ... and an American passport.

I had put Chad on the bus to Anchorage with no more than what he had been wearing in his sleeping bag.

It had been roughly thirty-five hours since Chad had walked up the stairs onto that bus. He had probably fallen asleep moments after taking his seat, but there was no doubt that he had discovered his predicament by now. Unfortunately, with the layover day we had spent in Whitehorse, the servicing needed on my Jeep, and the long drive to Anchorage, there was no way we could get there any sooner than the five-day meeting time we had arranged at the start. Chad was clearly on his own, attempting to cross an international border without pants or passport.

A number of questions flooded my mind. How would the officials at the Canadian-American border react to this young, pants-less man who claimed to be an American? What did the person sitting next to Chad think of him? I imagined him explaining his predicament to a little old lady with blue hair.

And assuming Chad did make it to Anchorage, what would he do for three days while he waited for us to arrive? Where would he be? How would we locate him? (This was well before the days of email and text messaging.) And perhaps more to the point, would I have to drive to Toledo, Ohio and explain to Chad's mother how I came to have not only her son's passport, but also his pants?

Thought-provoking as these questions were, there was nothing for us to do but throw his stuff into the Jeep and leave for Anchorage.

We heard an interesting story on Alaskan radio later than day. A retired couple driving the Alaska Highway in their RV had pulled over at a gas station, and while the husband was gassing up, his wife had stepped out of the rig to give herself and the couple's wiener dog a chance to stretch their legs. Moments later, a bald eagle had swooped down out of nowhere, grabbed the tiny wiener dog in its talons, and flew off with it. I pictured poor Chad sitting on the side of the road after having been kicked off the bus for his obscene pants-less behaviour. I hoped he was too big for the resident eagles.

We drove into Anchorage on the appointed day and began easing our way through the city toward the youth hostel. As we drove down one major street, my attention was grabbed by the oddest of sights: there in my rearview mirror was a disheveled-looking man clad in white, wearing Stanfield's long underwear, a red North Face Gore-Tex jacket, and a pair of Teva sandals. He was running up the middle of the road behind the Jeep waving his arms frantically and shouting at the top of his lungs.

Had it been any other day, in any other city, I would have kept driving. But this was Anchorage, and the crazed-looking man in long johns was clearly our long-lost friend from Ohio.

I parked the Jeep, and as I climbed from the driver's seat, a tearful Chad ran up and embraced me. He was crying, babbling like a three-year-old who had lost and then found his favourite stuffed animal companion. I gave him a few manly pats on the back. He certainly did look rough! A very relieved Chad sat down on the curb beside us and recounted the last five days of his life.

As it turns out, no one had ever asked to see his bus ticket. Apparently the line of people I had shoved him into at the bus depot had already checked their tickets, and as soon as he was on the bus, he had promptly fallen asleep. He had continued sleeping through the border crossing and, oddly enough, no one had bothered to wake him there. One would think a man traveling in long underwear would merit special attention from the border guards, but who am I to question their authority?

Upon arrival in Anchorage, Chad had walked across town to the youth hostel. He had somehow convinced the manager that he was a harmless university student from Ohio who had accidentally left all his belongings in Whitehorse, and was waiting for the arrival of his travel companions, who had his clothes, money, and ID. The manager not only believed him, but had even extended him credit pending the arrival of said travel companions. As for food, he had been living off of six cans of tuna that some Danish travelers staying at the youth hostel had given him.

Happy as a clam at high tide—or rather, a man in Anchorage with both pants and passport—Chad finished his story and offered to show us around town.

*Wayne has returned to the Far North several times since that first trip. Other memorable adventures include a paddling trip along the Yukon River from Carmacks to Dawson City, a road trip north along the Dempster Highway to Inuvik, and an October weekend "jaunt" from Calgary, Alberta to Great Slave Lake, NWT that ended in a blizzard. He currently lives in Ottawa, Ontario, where he teaches at a French Immersion Elementary School and runs a small publishing company called Stonecutter Press. Sadly, he has lost touch with Chad, who will perhaps read a copy of this book and send Wayne an email at **stonecut@hotmail.com**.*

Pirate Bear

Some bears like to eat fish...

By Matt Jackson

Northern Ontario has been a spawning ground for many great fishing tales over the years. Some of the stories are even true, like the quiet morning in July 2006 when Elliot Lake guide and outfitter Marty Descoteaux had his fishing boat hijacked by a black bear.

The day had started like many others at that time of year: Descoteaux was out in his sixteen-and-a-half-foot fibreglass Spincraft, scouting Esten Lake for an upcoming trip with some American clients. He had just completed a large loop with a downrigger, and had already netted a twelve-pound lake trout. He decided to make one more pass before motoring back to where his vehicle was waiting.

According to Descoteaux, the Elliot Lake vicinity is God's country—one of northern Ontario's most idyllic fishing locales. The region's deep lakes and crystalline rivers hold a variety of fighting fish to tempt any serious angler: huge brook trout, aggressive lake trout, acrobatic smallmouth bass, and large stocks of northern pike and walleye. Set amidst the fragrant pine forests and picturesque granite hills of Canada's Precambrian Shield, Descoteaux feels privileged to introduce his guests to Elliot Lake country ... and watch them return year after year.

On that quiet morning in early July, however, Descoteaux was by himself. As he turned his boat around for the final loop, he saw a large black bear swimming across the lake a few dozen meters to the left of his boat. Although the boat's path appeared to intersect the swimming bear's trajectory, the seasoned outfitter remained unconcerned. He figured the bear would spook and start swimming in the opposite direction as soon as he saw the skiff. Thus, the longtime guide continued trolling, the bear continued swimming, and the boat continued puttering along its intersecting path.

As the seemingly oblivious bear continued swimming toward the skiff, Descoteaux's anticipation grew. How would the bear react when it saw the boat? What would it do?

The skiff was almost on top of the bear when, to the guide's utter disbelief, the bear reached its paws forward and clamped onto the side of his boat.

Descoteaux hadn't expected that to happen.

He grabbed a paddle and took a few swipes at the bear, trying to dislodge it from its precarious perch. The bear, apparently taking exception to the guide's less-than-polite greeting, went completely ballistic. It growled, snapped its teeth, and a few seconds later hoisted itself aboard the still-moving skiff. With nowhere to go, Descoteaux abandoned his hijacked ship by diving overboard.

The shore was not far, and after he had reached it, Descoteaux turned to watch a strange scene unfold. The bear was still in his boat—snooping around, sniffing at its contents, no doubt looking for the fish the guide had caught.

A minute later, the inquisitive bear accidentally hit the boat's throttle.

The engine roared to life and the boat surged forward. As the craft picked up speed, the bear appeared to panic, but before it could decide what to do, the boat had veered to one side and rammed at full speed into a rocky outcrop that protruded from the shore. The grounded boat stopped with a *bang!*... but the bear kept on going. It flew ass-first out of the boat and landed with a thud on the rocky ground.

That was enough for the bear. It got up and ran into the forest without so much as looking back.

Unfortunately, that was not the end of Descoteaux's misadventure. The boat was still at full throttle, and somehow managed to work itself free of the shoreline. The disbelieving guide watched as it circled the bay unmanned for the next twenty minutes, until it finally ran aground, destroying the engine in the process. It had beached itself on the far side of the bay, so Descoteaux had to strip down to his long underwear and swim for more than half a kilometer to retrieve it.

When he later called his insurance company, Descoteaux learned that it considered bear hijacking to be an "Act of God." He was thus forced to ante up three thousand dollars to have his boat repaired—quite clearly an un-*bear*-able cost.

For his part, Descoteaux has made peace with Esten Lake's pirate bear. In fact, he claims he's somewhat disappointed that another equally plausible scenario didn't unfold. If the curious bear hadn't accidentally hit the boat's throttle, it's quite likely the skiff would have continued on its original course, straight onto the popular and well-used main section of Esten Lake. And if that had happened, local fishermen would have been treated to an unprecedented sight: a fibreglass fishing boat with a downrigger being expertly piloted across the lake by a black bear.

I wonder if anybody would have believed them.

Matt Jackson is the president of Summit Studios and author of the award-winning book The Canada Chronicles: A Four-year Hitchhiking Odyssey. *He has encountered many bears on his wilderness forays, but has never been hijacked by one. He hopes that trend will continue.*

For more information about his fishing charters, visit Marty Descoteaux at www.elliotlakeoutfitters.com.

What Your Parents Don't Teach You

Learning (quickly) about childcare at a Nepalese orphanage.

By Conor Grennan

In the orphanage, the bedroom for the younger boys had the two youngest sleeping on the floor, curled up together on a carefully laid pile of blankets and towels. Next to them, an ancient king-sized bed that stood just a foot off the ground held four more boys. The bed dwarfed them like tadpoles in a bathtub.

The silence felt strange to me—just twenty minutes earlier, noise had thundered and rolled out of the room in waves, the kind of indignant howling usually reserved for confrontations with riot police. It had been about as loud as a high school production of *West Side Story*, and had played out with similar pitched enthusiasm. Sleep, however, was the ultimate peacemaker; arguments and fights and accusations had evaporated. Four children who had minutes earlier been bickering over space on a pillow now lay with limbs intertwined, unconsciously huddled together in the Nepali winter, their dark-haired heads arranged on the blanket like bowling balls on a rack.

The two boys sleeping on the makeshift bed on the floor had yet to grow out of the bedwetting stage—hence the temporary segregation. Tonight, though, we hoped to change that. Chris, a German volunteer at the orphanage, had an idea that involved—as crazy as it sounded to me—carrying them to the toilet in the middle of the night. The theory was that this would control the "where and when," so to speak, and help boost their confidence. It was worth a try. At least it seemed a remarkably simple plan to execute.

And no doubt it *would* have been remarkably simple to execute for someone who had even the slightest clue about basic child care. Which, alas, I did not.

*   *   *

My decision to volunteer at an orphanage in Nepal was made, like so many of my life's grand decisions, without a great deal of forethought. "Hey, this sounds interesting!" my brain said before it went off to hibernate, leaving my body to cope with the implementation phase. I wasn't being completely naïve; I understood that it would require certain skills with children to work in an orphanage. It only occurred to me later, however, that I probably did not actually possess those skills.

In the final days before I left for Nepal, I had to remind myself that I had *chosen* to volunteer. "I *want* to volunteer," I would say aloud, panting into a paper bag. "This is *my choice*." And it was true: nobody had pressured me into it. Indeed, a number of friends had even (gently) suggested that caring for orphans in the developing world might not be exactly what I was cut out for. And yet, for this very reason, I remained convinced that I *had* to do it. I'd just celebrated my thirtieth cushy year, and I felt the need to see and experience the worlds of those I considered less fortunate than myself.

Standing outside the gate of the orphanage, in a small village south of Kathmandu, as I listened to the madness and hubbub of the eighteen children inside, it dawned on me that I didn't actually want this experience at all. What I wanted was to *tell* people I'd volunteered in an orphanage. Yet I here I was, utterly and desperately unprepared. This was not how I had imagined this moment. I had imagined it as a moment of triumph: the American arrives to save the orphans! The soundtrack featured bugles. I would stride in, equal parts superior and magnanimous.

Instead I felt neither of those things. I felt terrified. And yet there was nothing else for me to do but push open the front gate and step into the garden.

As it happens, wondering what you're supposed to do in an orphanage is like wondering what you're supposed to do at the Running of the Bulls in Spain: you work it out pretty quickly. I closed the gate behind me and stared for the first time at a sea of wide-eyed Nepalese children. I took a deep breath to calm down and introduce myself. Before I could utter a word, however, I had been set upon—charged at, overrun, jumped on—by a herd of laughing children. Just like the bulls in Pamplona.

*   *   *

Chris nodded toward the clock. It was 10:30 p.m. "Shall we?" he said, setting down his mug of milk tea and rising from his chair.

There must be dozens of books on how to teach young children not to wet the bed. Sadly, we didn't have one. Forging ahead, we creaked open the door to the bedroom and gazed into the gloom. The children were not merely asleep; they had dropped from the world entirely. Their little pajama-clad bodies were splayed dramatically across the bed and floor, giving the impression of a team of tiny acrobats frozen in mid-routine.

We tiptoed in, though we needn't have worried about waking them. A helicopter landing on the roof wouldn't have stirred them. As we crept over to the youngest boys on the floor, Chris whispered that he would take Rashmi to the toilet first. When he returned, I would bring Himal. He scooped up his little man and tiptoed out. I heard the light click on in the bathroom, then the telltale sounds of things going according to plan. He clicked off the light a minute later and reentered the room, carrying a semi-conscious Rashmi, who was lazily rubbing his sleepy eyes. Chris laid him back down.

"Right—off you go," Chris said to me, nodding at the dozing Himal as he pulled the blankets up over his charge. Following his example, I gathered Himal in my arms and carried him to the bathroom. *This should be easy*, I thought.

*   *   *

I've often been asked what it is that one does all day in an orphanage. "Take care of them" rarely satisfies the questioner.

"Yes, but what do you actually *do*?" It's as if they envision eighteen children lined up in three precise rows awaiting instructions.

There is one group, however, that never asks this question: parents. Their questions are more specific and invariably begin with, "How the *hell* do you..." followed by a predicate such as, "...get them ready for school?"

Good question, parents. The children all wear identical blue uniforms, which are often thrown together into a large unruly pile after washing. Inevitably the pile must be sorted. Unfortunately, "sorting" is not necessarily a four-year-old's forte. Inside the bedroom a veritable tornado of school uniforms is unleashed. Inevitably, little hyperactive Nanda will mistakenly pick out the trousers of one of the older boys, and immediately thrust his legs into the giant pair of pants. Tears of frustration well up in his eyes because he is having trouble getting them on; the trouble being, of course, that the zipper starts at his chin. You walk in just in time to see him zipping them up over his face and attempting to fasten the belt around his head. Wrong trousers, little dude.

Eventually, each one of the sixteen boys and two girls will locate and put on (with a little help) his or her proper clothes, and they will line up and head off to school, happily waving goodbye. Then, more often than not, they will come marching right back a half-hour later, reporting that the teachers did not bother to show up again or the Maoist rebels (who control most of the country) have called a general strike and schools will remain closed, along with everything else. In those instances, we divide the children into small groups and tutor them the best we can.

We play games like Junior Scrabble to help them with their spelling. To illustrate my expertise in this subject area, I helped seven-year-old Chakshu arrange his letters into the word "sperm," defining it as "a kind of whale" (and that's all). The memory card game Farmyard Snap, which the younger kids were fond of and in which they were surprisingly skilled, forced me to concentrate fully to avoid complete humiliation. The object of the game was to help them learn the names of the animals in the pictures, but often it became a lesson in the desperate lengths adult American males will go to in order to avoid defeat.

*   *   *

I have to admit that Chris's plan to wake the two smallest children and take them to the toilet ran contrary to every one of my instincts; it took an enormous amount of effort to get them into bed in the first place, and it seemed like folly to disturb them. Mornings were chaotic, but at least the children were single-minded in their purpose of finding their school uniforms. Bedtime, by way of contrast, completely baffled them every single night. It never failed. The children would finish their evening meal of daal bhat, a rice dish with curried vegetables and a weak lentil soup poured over it, and become instantly energized.

When I'd first envisaged working in an orphanage, bedtime was a kind of serene *Sound of Music* type of scene—little boys and girls curling happily into bed and quietly dozing off after singing to each other. It was not like that. It was like a lone sheepdog trying to corral a flock of sheep, except *these* sheep giggled madly and wanted nothing more than to sprint back and forth through the house in their underwear.

Putting the older kids to bed was simpler, but came with its own perils. I had just said goodnight to them one evening when eight-year-old Giri suddenly asked, "Brother, in your country, do you eat meat?" (The Nepalese address each other as "brother" or "sister" as a term of respect.)

"Sure," I said. "Chicken, pig…"

"Goat?"

"Umm, not really—more like sheep, cow…"

"*Cow?*" This was quickly translated for the others, and I suddenly had the attention of an entire room of young Hindu boys. "*Eat cow?*"

"Well, only sometimes … you know, come to think of it, it's really more my *friends* that eat …"

"You eat *God*, Brother?" came an incredulous voice from the other side of the room.

"No, of course not … I mean, he's not *our* God, you know …"

"Cow *not* God?!"

Yikes! "No—cow God, cow God, but in America and Europe…"

"Why do you eat God, Brother?" demanded Giri.

I was getting desperate. "Well, cow not really *God* God, and you have no idea how it tastes because you haven't tried it—it's really good!"

There was a loud thump as somebody's jaw hit the floor, then complete silence.

"Uh ... okay ... well, goodnight boys!"

I backed out of the room, slapped blindly at the light switch, and hurriedly pulled the door closed behind me.

*   *   *

I have since been assured, by those in the know, that taking a child to the toilet in the middle of the night is an accepted method of teaching them to overcome the bedwetting hurdle. I have to assume, however, that it is most effective when at least one of two conditions is met: (1) the child in question actually wakes up at some point during the urination process, or (2) the adult who is taking the child is not a complete idiot.

In my case, neither condition was met. In fact, the entire incident later became known among my fellow volunteers simply as "The Fiasco."

The problem itself was deceptively simple: Himal wore a full teddy-bear suit (like a pajama jumpsuit) to bed. I don't know how many of you had one of those when you were little—I know I did—but as you may also know, they can be somewhat problematic to undo. The zipper on this particular teddy-bear suit ran from Himal's left ankle up to his neck.

This problem alone would not have been insurmountable. However, when combined with the fact that Himal never really woke up during the whole process—well, I had a bit of trouble. Himal was fast asleep and limp as a rag doll, which meant it was necessary to hold him up with one arm and unzip his jumpsuit with the other. Have you ever tried to unzip something like that with one hand? It's not easy, I can assure you.

I stood at the toilet with Himal for many long minutes, trying desperately to "position" him correctly. But his legs kept giving out like they were made of yarn. To make matters worse, the floor was wet, so I had to hoist him up and attempt to slide a towel under his feet. This was more difficult than it sounds—since my hands were occupied, I was only using my feet to push the towel into place. I finally got the towel in position and lowered Himal back down.

I guess I was distracted while trying to position the towel, because I ended up lowering the little guy *into* the toilet.

Up to that moment, Himal had been asleep, his head hanging limply against his chest. He woke up with an adorably huge yawn, his sleepy eyes cracking open just in time to see that *somebody* was trying to *flush him down the toilet.*

His legs shot out like a gymnast and locked onto the rim of the bowl, which startled me enough that I nearly dropped him. It must have been a hell of a way to wake up. I pulled him up and back from the toilet, and he craned his neck around to see who was holding him. When he saw me he let out a sleepy little giggle, and then, remarkably, fell back to sleep.

Unfortunately, there was still the business of zipping him back up. If I thought *unzipping* his suit with one hand was hard, zipping him back up proved to be virtually impossible. In a final desperate effort, I stood him up in the bathroom sink and pinned him against the wall with my head, which freed both of my hands.

And that's when Chris walked in to see what was taking so long.

I don't know what it looked like I was doing. I do know that I had a four-year-old pinned to the wall with my head, my hands wrapped around his ankle. In his limp state, Himal was slumped over the top of my head, so I was kind of wearing him like a hat. It sure as hell didn't *look* like I was taking him for a pee. Chris must have wondered if I had, in fact, even understood what we were trying to do. He stood in the doorway, speechless.

I didn't know what to say either, so I just said the first thing that came to me. It was something that, given the evidence, probably didn't need saying at all:

"Little help?"

*   *   *

As time passed, I got better at things. I got better at sorting multiple sets of identical clothes simultaneously and passing them to the appropriate child. I got better at tutoring them, selecting vocabulary that was more pertinent to their lives. And I became less concerned about beating four-year-olds at Farmyard Snap. I stopped eating meat almost entirely in Nepal, just to be safe, and learned more about Hinduism. I got better at just about everything, which, considering I had started off at such a low level (flushing a child down the toilet) perhaps isn't such a surprise.

Three months later I said goodbye to the children. It was harder than I thought it would be. I had imagined it as a tearful moment—mostly for the children. I figured the tears would be gushing from their eyes as they begged me not to go. As for me, I would saunter out confidently, knowing that I had made the world just a little bit better, feeling equal parts satisfied and relieved that it was over.

But that's not how it happened. Instead, it was me hugging them with a little more urgency than I could have anticipated. I did not want to leave. I boarded the plane anyway, taking a window seat on the right-hand side so that I could see the Himalayas for the last time.

I took comfort in knowing that in a matter of hours, I would be able to tell my friends I'd volunteered in a Nepalese orphanage. And that would probably sound super cool—that's what this was all about, right?

Even before we had touched down in London, I made the decision to go back to Nepal. Not just to volunteer this time, but to start an orphanage. Nepal is among the poorest countries in the world, and is recovering from a decade-long civil war. There are over two hundred thousand refugees in Kathmandu alone. The United Nations named the plight of conflict-plagued children in Nepal as one of the *Top Ten Stories the World Should Hear More About* in 2006. In short, there is no shortage of children who have nobody to care for them.

Six months later I kept my promise: I returned to Nepal to live. I opened a new orphanage for trafficked children, and I take care of them every day.

I know what you're thinking: "Haven't the children suffered enough?" The answer, clearly, is "No." Still, for the sake of the children, let's hope that I'm a bit better at it this time around.

Conor Grennan helped to found a new Nepalese orphanage in 2006. He lived there for more than a year and successfully tracked down several of the children he had cared for during his previous sojourn. His non-profit organization, Next Generation Nepal, *not only cares for trafficked children but helps to reunite them with their parents. You can learn more about NGN by visiting* **www.nextgenerationnepal.org**.

A Jamaican Dance

I am Shopping Guru, King of the Bargain.
Hear me roar...

By Nick Klenske

The moment I hopped out of the taxi, a blast of thick, moist tropical air hit my face. I heard people and saw a blur of commotion, yet I felt somehow displaced. Was I sleepwalking? In a trance? I floated, separated from the scene before me, awash in the faint yet unmistakable stench of stale sweat. The sun seemed to set as the light dimmed into a faux-dusk of dancing shadows cast by tangled palm leaves.

"Here we are," said my wife Kara with a smile.

We were at the Ocho Rios Market, and it was time to shop. Kara and I were soon engulfed in a swarm of shop owners offering us coffee, crafts, and the occasional Ziploc baggie of cannabis.

"Come with me, mon," said one of them, his mellow and soothing voice rising from the madness. "I will be your friend and show you the shops. I will bring you to my shop and show you my things. If you like what you see, then we make a deal. If you don't like what you see, no hard feelings. You just give me a dollar for my guidance and we are still friends. Irie, yea?"

Without giving it a second thought, we followed the man into the market and began our quest for the perfect Jamaican souvenir.

"This is my shop," said our man as we stopped at a shady corner tucked into the far end of the market. "Take some time. See what you like. Then we can make a deal."

His shop consisted of a small corner about the size of a hall closet, overflowing with an array of goods. Coasters, multicolored masks, and smooth wooden jewelry cluttered the shelves. Fierce African elephants and five-foot-tall giraffes spilled from the entrance and onto the pavement. It was a souvenir-sucker's treasure trove.

"How much for the carved male and female busts?" I inquired.

"The bookends," he clarified. "They are sixty dollars. But for you, my friend, I will give you a deal and charge you only fifty." He gently rested his hand on my shoulder for an added touch of scripted sincerity.

I looked up and gave him a sly smile. *Let the bartering begin*, I thought. It was time to dance.

"Hmm," I replied, folding my arms and feigning frustration. "How about the coasters?"

"These coasters? You like the coasters? They are quite nice. They have a Jamaican ten-dollar piece engraved in them," he said enthusiastically. "The coasters are forty dollars, but for you I will gladly take ten dollars off."

Not a bad deal, but not a good deal either, and by no means were the coasters what I wanted. I wanted the bookends. It was my move. I had to tread cautiously and attempt to read his mind. *How low will he go? What is his breaking point?* These are the critical pressure points any skilled negotiator must determine.

Of course, doubt is the champion negotiator's nemesis. It's always spitting negative thoughts: *He's reading you like a book. You're going to stumble. Ha! He deals with tourists like you everyday. He'll eat you for breakfast. You haven't got a chance.*

Then confidence rallies: *No. You have the skills of a champion shopper. You are the man, Nick. You are the man. Now shop, dammit, shop like the man you are!*

"Humph!" I grunted with feigned impatience.

"Look, mon, you are my friend and a guest in my country," the man said as he placed his hand on his heart. "I will give you the coasters—and this—for only thirty dollars." He reached behind his back and presented to me a wooden goblet the size of a shot glass.

"See?" he said as he endearingly caressed its side. "Nice shot glass."

"Humph." I tried to downplay my interest while wiping away the sweat beading on my forehead. I bit my lower lip, perhaps a little too hard. This was intense.

"The coasters and a shot glass?" I asked. "But what about my wife? I can't expect her to sit idly by while I enjoy my shot of rum crème, now can I?" I chuckled.

"Of course not! I should have known: you are a gentleman," he said with a false gesture of politeness. "Since I am a gentleman too, I will sell you the coasters and two shot glasses for only thirty dollars. How does that sound? Irie?"

Of course, I didn't want the coasters. I wanted the bookends. It was time to bring this dance full circle. It was time for a twirl.

"How much for the bookends again?"

"The bookends? Thirty dollars!" he answered quickly, carefully placing the coasters back on the shelf without missing a beat. He knew what I was after, and I knew what he was after. It was a race to the finish.

"Can I buy just one?" I asked, trying to sound naïve. "How much for just one of the carved heads?"

"No! No! They are bookends. A set. A man and a woman. They would be lonely if they were separated," he joked half-heartedly. "How about this, mon. I know you like the bookends. I will give you the best deal in all of Jamaica."

In a hushed voice, he continued, "If you give me thirty dollars for the bookends, then I give you the two shot glasses…" He paused, peered cautiously over his shoulder while licking his lips, swallowed, and then whispered, "…for *free*."

Now that was a deal. But I was rather enjoying my luck and the macho feeling of my ego being stroked, so I arrogantly pushed for more.

"We're both college students and we're a bit short on cash. How much to buy just one shot glass?"

"No! No!" he shouted anxiously, showing his frustration.

I had him.

"I tell you what," he pleaded. "Here's a deal. The best deal. My final offer. I can do no more." He quickly added, "I usually don't make such deals, but you are a good friend and a skilled negotiator, so I do this only for you. I sell you the bookends and give you the two shot glasses for only twenty-five dollars."

He said I had skills! I gave him a smile and held out my hand. "You've got yourself a deal."

Money was exchanged, the bookends tenderly wrapped, and Kara and I began to make our way to the exit. I was perspiring with pride, enjoying a shopper's high. *Nick, you sure know how to drive a bargain*, I thought to myself. *You got yourself a hell of a deal.* I was a shopper with superhuman shopping skills. I was a man's man. I felt a sudden, primal urge to puff out my chest, grunt, and scratch with reckless abandon. I am Nick, Shopping Guru, King of the Bargain. Hear me roar.

Just then, a merchant emerged from his stall carrying a set of bookends. A male and a female set similar to the pair I had just bought. Very similar, in fact. Perhaps on the verge of *identical*.

"I give you the best deal, mon," he began. "Because you are my good friend, I sell you these two handcrafted bookends for only ten dollars."

Kara just laughed.

"I still have my two shot glasses," I mumbled.

Nick Klenske is an attorney, freelance writer, and travel consultant. Learn more about Nick's travels by visiting his web site, **www.klensketravel.com.**

Newlyweds on the Trapline

*Romance can be painfully elusive in the
Alaskan wilderness.*

By Michelle Bruce

Y ou have to hit the target dead on, or you're going to do it again.
Do you understand?" That was my husband Ben, telling me
in no uncertain terms that bear spray, jingle bells, and singing
the Beach Boys wouldn't cut it out here. This was for real. This
was Alaska. And Alaska has bears. Lots of bears. Today he was
determined to teach me the finer points of handling a shotgun.

Ben crossed through the woods that circled our small canvas
tent, which was hunkered between a stand of trees in the remote
Alaskan wilderness. He took an old dog food bag, drew a large
bullseye on it, and nailed it to a tree. As I backed up twenty-five
yards and considered taking aim, he explained for the hundredth
time that if a bear came into camp I needed to know how to use the
shotgun. If a bear decided on visiting our camp for a free lunch,
buckshot might be the only thing that would deter him.

I felt pretty sure I knew what I was doing. As a kid in 4-H, I
had gone to the shooting range and shot at the clay pigeons. So
what if I was twelve at the time? It was like riding a bike, right? I
nuzzled the gun into my shoulder, looked down the barrel, took a
deep breath, exhaled, and pulled the trigger.

BOOM!

The shotgun kicked like a horse and I winced. "Damn thing almost took my shoulder off," I whined.

"Shoot again," Ben hollered. "You didn't hit the middle. If that was a bear, you just pissed him off."

I hesitated. The shotgun's kick had hurt. Ben saw the look on my face and said, "A bear will hurt a hell of a lot more! Now, shoot again."

There was no way I was missing this time. I took aim, shot again, and hit the bullseye dead on.

"That's my girl! I knew you had it in you."

I smiled, proud of myself—and very grateful I didn't have to shoot again. My shoulder was still aching. Living on a remote Alaska trapline had its rewards, but it sure had its share of challenges, too. This was just one of the many new skills I had to learn to be prepared for daily living in the wilderness.

Ben and I were newlyweds, living one hundred and thirty kilometers from the nearest town. We'd moved to a remote trapline to mush dogs and live a simpler life. It was wonderful, but it was a huge change from the life I was used to. There was a time, just four years prior, when I had worked as a traveling college counselor for my alma mater outside of St. Louis. I traveled the country staying in bed and breakfasts; my coffee came from the local Starbucks; and going out meant wearing heels and miniskirts. Now my coffee was percolated on a woodstove, and going out meant using the outhouse.

It was a change that I was ready for, and gladly accepted. I had always dreamed of living like my grandmother had lived—as a pioneer woman. Alaska was my opportunity to do just that! Ben and I met in Bethel, Alaska, a small town eight hundred kilometers west of Anchorage. I was an elementary school teacher and Ben taught pre-school. We were surprised to have so much in common, and after just a few dates we had a pretty good idea that this was it! We shared a passion for living life, and craved change and adventure. Many of our first dates consisted of me following Ben on my snow machine as he mushed his dog team. We'd camp out for the night, and then mush back into town. After dating for a year, we got married in an outdoor ceremony, where I got to mush the dog team down the aisle.

Ben and I both dreamed of living remotely, so the trapline was a perfect fit; there would be no running water, no electricity, and no heated cabin. Instead, we settled in with our dog team, an eight man Arctic tent, and a large woodstove. The Alaskan wilderness was on our front stoop, with no interference. No cellphones, no television, no neighbors to make unexpected drop-ins, and no computers to distract us. For a couple of newlyweds, it was the perfect setup. Can you think of a more dramatic way to get to know your husband than by living in a day-to-day survival situation?

We spent our days caring for the dogs, trapping for our income, and hunting for our own food. We walked hand-in-hand down the frozen creek bed to look for fox tracks, spent afternoons panning for gold, snuggled into our sleeping bags when a blizzard set in, and hiked the nearby mountains looking for game.

On the days my husband was out trapping, I would see to the domestic duties around the camp: washing laundry, cooking meals, and so on. I enjoyed these activities, as they weren't mundane when done at camp; I saw it as a challenge. We had to haul water from the creek to drink, wash, and cook with. That, in and of itself, took a long time. Never mind that you had to heat it over the woodstove, adding an hour to an already lengthy process.

Doing laundry was the toughest, because you had to haul several pails of water for each wash. I began to get my arm strength up and could soon carry a forty-five-pound bucket of water the fifty meters back to our tent without having to stop for a break. Some might find this tedious, but the truth is, the day-to-day chores gave me a great sense of accomplishment because of the extra effort required to do them. At night my husband and I slept well, as we had spent our days outside and had worked hard.

All my friends joked before we left that I'd return the next summer pregnant, since we'd have nothing better to do on the trapline than fool around. Boy, were they wrong! I'll never forget my naïvety about being a new wife. I figured we'd have plenty of time, too. But with no indoor plumbing it was tricky to bathe. Our official policy was to shower once a week, whether we needed it or not. And you can bet we did!

We were very lucky to have received a small portable shower as a wedding gift from some friends. Those friends certainly knew what a useful gift was. The shower had a tank that you placed on top of the woodstove and heated to the desired temperature. Then you used a pump to pressurize the tank, and finally used a small nozzle to spray yourself down while standing in a small basin next to the stove. You could muster about twenty seconds of water pressure before you had to pump again.

We bathed inside the tent because at minus thirty degrees Celsius outside, the water would have frozen too quickly. (Not to mention the fact that it would have been a dreadful experience to be naked out there.) It took at least two hours for the large tank of water to heat up to a warm thirty-five degrees. Plus, it required almost twelve liters of water to be hauled from the creek, which meant that bathing became an afternoon event.

My maid of honor had thrown me a very nice shower, where I had received several sexy nighties. One cold day while my husband was out running the dogs and checking traps, I decided it was time I pulled one of these nighties out of the bottom of the trunk to surprise him when he got home. I spent the afternoon hauling extra water so I could bathe, shave, and prepare for a special romantic night. I could hardly wait for him to pull up with the dogs. He would come home to find a hot, homemade meal on the table, the candles and lanterns lit, and his new wife wearing her finest lingerie.

This was what being newlyweds was all about! So what if it had been two months since we said our vows? We both knew that living on the trapline demanded some sacrifices, but tonight I'd make up for some of them.

When Ben pulled up with the dogs, I felt a sudden rush of excitement. Unfortunately, it was short lived.

Ben hollered from outside for me to get my gear on—he needed my help. The tone of his voice indicated that I shouldn't dawdle, so I quickly threw on my long johns, fleece bibs, down coat, hat, gloves, boots, and headlamp. I opened the door of the tent and saw my husband unleashing his sled bag. There was a dog nestled in it.

Without explanation, he told me to put up the remaining dogs quickly, then to clear the tent table. We were going to have to perform some surgery.

As it turned out, two of the younger dogs had stumbled onto a porcupine and were absolutely covered in quills. We'd have to give them shots to numb them and then remove the quills before they lodged further under the skin.

By the end of the evening we had removed over ninety quills from the dogs, and they were both resting peacefully by the fire. It had taken us about five hours to remove them all, and we were exhausted. Dinner was cold, and I was ready for bed. I peeled off my long johns, took a look at myself in the lingerie, and sighed. Our romantic evening was never even mentioned; I didn't have the heart to tell my husband what I had planned. I would prepare it all again another time.

The next time came about two weeks later. Again I hauled extra water for a shower and shave, prepared a scrumptious dinner, lit some candles, and donned my special nightie. This time I felt sure we'd have the nice evening I had planned.

Once again I felt a rush of excitement when Ben pulled up with the dogs. I peeked out of the tent, and Ben asked me to come and help put the dogs away. I wasn't worried, as he often asked for help. I dressed quickly and started for the door when I realized that Ben wasn't handling the dogs yet. He was still standing on the sled. Usually he had put two or three of them away by the time I got outside.

He had a large smile on his face and I was afraid my surprise was over. Yet his smile was mischievous. He was waiting for me to see something.

I took a closer look and realized that my husband's arm was covered in porcupine quills. He wasn't in too much pain, but it looked horrible! He'd shot a porcupine for dinner and had placed it on top of the sled bag. When he'd unexpectedly hit a tundra tussock, the sled tipped over, the porcupine fell off, and Ben had slid right into the damn thing.

Ben joked that it was the porcupine's last act of defiance. Little did he know that this porcupine was also keeping us from sharing a romantic night together. I spent the evening pulling over one hundred quills out of his arm.

Who would have thought porcupines could be such an effective form of birth control?

Michelle Bruce became a mother shortly after she and Ben moved to Florida, where there are substantially fewer porcupines.

Kancho Christmas

In Japan, Santa Claus is an endangered species.

By Jay Fitzsimmons

It seemed like a good idea at the time. I was a Canadian English teacher in the rural town of Uwa-cho, Japan, and Christmas was coming. Why not dress up as Santa Claus and visit the elementary schools where I taught? Santa is not an integral part of Japanese culture, and I figured it would be a fun way to bring North American Yuletide traditions to the schoolkids I had come to know.

With visions of smiling children singing Christmas carols, I found a Santa outfit at the town's bargain shop for the equivalent of four dollars. It was made of cheap red felt and ugly trim, but I guess you get what you pay for.

There are eight elementary schools in Uwa-cho. My goal was to visit each one in turn on different days, whenever my teaching load at the junior high school would permit. The first elementary school was Unomachi School.

Children can be remarkably astute, despite what some teachers might say after a bad day at work. Kids are certainly smart enough to figure out that "Santa," who is giving them a short Christmas-themed English lesson, is most likely Jay-sensei, the English teacher from Canada. I was one of only two white people who lived in town; the other was a reclusive Dutch sculptor who apparently lived in the hills, though I'd never met him. I figured the students would laugh a little at my silliness, but I didn't delude myself into thinking they would be excited by my visit.

I had purchased an old granny bike to ride around town when I first arrived in Japan, so I dressed in my Santa outfit and rode slowly to Unomachi Elementary School. More than a few people stopped to gawk—one old woman even got off a passing bus to take my picture. I felt like a small-town celebrity.

When I reached the school, I stopped to lock up my bike. The bike racks were next to the windows of the grade four classroom, and when I peeked inside, I could see a young boy looking very bored with whatever lesson was being taught. When he glanced outside, his face lit up. Through the glass I saw him yell, "SANTA!"

Good, I thought. *At least they know who I'm supposed to be.*

I was still in the process of locking my bike when the entire grade four class emptied from the school, charged outside, and swarmed me. Judging the time between the boy's exclamation and the arrival of the swarming mob, they could not have been formally dismissed by their teacher. They simply ran outside to meet Santa.

This surprised Santa.

Everywhere Santa looked, exultant children were asking him questions. ("HO HO HO!" is the perfect answer when you're dressed like Santa and don't understand what the kids are saying.) Some children were climbing up Santa's limbs trying to get onto his pillow-padded gut. Some were hugging Santa.

Still others were *kancho*-ing Santa.

According to Wikipedia at the time of writing, *kancho* is "a slang adoption of the Japanese word for enema." It entails one person (the *kancho*-er) bringing his or her hands together with index fingers extended (like a gun) and ramming said fingers between the butt cheeks of the second person (the *kancho*-ee). Although it is not mentioned in any "Teach English in Japan" brochure of which I am aware, it is not uncommon for teachers to be *kancho*-ed in elementary schools.

Santa, who had teaching tools in one hand, a bicycle lock in the other, and children climbing all over him, was not prepared for *kancho*.

"*Kancho-dame!*" Santa frantically shouted, telling the children he did not want any small Japanese fingers jammed between his buttocks. But Santa's pleas were in vain. Slowed by the weight of children on his limbs, he could not turn around fast enough to stop *kancho* attacks to his backside. Just like the raptors in the movie *Jurassic Park*, you could stare at one child to ensure he would not *kancho* you, but another would sneak in from the side with a successful *kancho* attack.

Soon several classrooms had emptied into the schoolyard, and students from all grades were *kancho*-ing Santa and bombarding him with incoherent (to him) questions. Teachers were leaning against the school, laughing at Santa's plight.

Finally, Santa managed to free himself from the grasps and *kancho*s of his smiling young assailants. He went on to lead the grade six class in some pleasant Christmas carols, and with a somewhat sore backside, left the school shortly thereafter.

When I got home I discovered that the *kancho*s had impacted me deeply—they had left a gaping hole in the butt area of my felt Santa pants. I had thought they felt a little drafty.

I tried to buy replacement pants at the bargain store, but they were sold out. Realizing it could be considered scandalous for me to visit the town's other elementary schools wearing pants with no backside, I decided Santa's tour of Uwa-cho's schools was finished for the year, after visiting only one school out of eight.

And that is how the students of Unomachi Elementary School ruined Christmas for the rest of the children of Uwa-cho. (To any former students of mine, I'm just kidding ... and congratulations on your ability to read this book).

It is also why, after returning to Canada, I instinctively clench my butt cheeks every time I see Santa Claus surrounded by children at a shopping mall.

Jay Fitzsimmons is a biology major who is currently working on his Ph.D. at the University of Ottawa. He has buns of steel.

Bear Scare

Who is more scared of whom?

By Glenn Kletke

Take my word for it: it's not something that's fun to think about. When you're planning a backpacking trip to the Canadian Rockies, the possibility of coming face to snout with a grizzly bear is suddenly very real, and it will always be at the bottom of your list of "things to experience firsthand." In fact, a close encounter with a grizzly bear would undoubtedly top your list for being at the bottom of the list.

So if you're anything like me, you *don't* think about it. You think about soaring peaks, wildflower meadows in bloom, and endless vistas—not about that little excerpt you read in, "How to Protect Yourself from Dangerous Predators."

And forget about watching any wilderness documentaries. I guarantee that in the month before you leave, there will be one featuring a great, toothy hulk with that telltale hump on its back, sprinting like greased lightning through tall meadow grass as the sunlight turns its fur to glints of silver. At any other time, this program would fill you with awe; a month before you leave, it will probably make you hug your toilet bowl and retch.

The truth had to be faced, of course. My two sons and I eventually found ourselves standing at the trailhead with great anticipation, our backpacks filled with three days' worth of supplies, one can of bear spray, three sleeping bags, a can of bear spray, one large tent, and … did I mention the can of bear spray?

I purchased the bear spray in a Rod & Gun store as the three of us made our long drive westward from our home in Ottawa, Ontario. The clerk had praised the product as the ultimate bear deterrent and told us it would almost guarantee against an attack. As the father, my role was that of responsible guide, and I was determined to show my sons how to handle themselves in all wilderness situations. The clerk carefully read me the operating instructions (a long list of warnings that I had forgotten by the time we left the store) and showed me how to release the canister's safety lock for instant use.

Three days later we were standing at the trailhead, preparing for a beautiful climb through the upper meadows of Waterton Lakes National Park. This small park in the southwestern corner of Alberta (adjacent to Montana's Glacier National Park) is renowned for its incredible alpine beauty and has a reputation for being slightly—*gulp!*—bear-infested.

The first few hours went like clockwork. Matt, John, and I hiked up a steep slope of switchbacks through the forest. We eventually reached the first meadows full of blooming bear grass, a tall white plant that when growing in bunches looks like a field of cotton candy sticks. Then we entered back into the dark forest for another kilometer or two before the trees finally disappeared for good.

It was at this point that interesting things began to happen.

Matt, who had absolutely no interest in the bear spray, was a seventeen-year-old completely devoted to his new video camera— he was constantly recording short, self-narrated sequences to produce (later, he hoped) a documentary to surpass anything the nature and wildlife networks could offer. He kept shooting into the dark pines and repeating, like a chant or endless litany, "No bear here. No bear here."

John, who was fifteen, was eager to prove himself strong and fearless, and had already replaced me as leader on the trail; he told me to pass the bear spray to him in the event it might suddenly be needed. As for myself, the scent of pine needles and the swirl of sunlight through the trees had relaxed me to the point of forgetting that bears and bear spray even exist.

"Now, look at this," said Matt into his camera. "This is really interesting."

I stopped to look at what he was shooting. It was a large, soft paw print in the middle of the trail. The pad and the formation of the toes (or was that claws?) left no doubt as to what kind of animal had been sharing our trail.

John was impressed. He checked the outside of my pack to make certain the spray was easily accessible. I assured my boys that the print could be days, maybe even weeks old.

Fifteen minutes later, Matt was talking into his camera again. "Now this is something rare and impressive. Looks like bear crap to me." As he began zooming in on the pile, he suddenly said, "Holy smokes! It's still steaming!"

John raced back to get a closer look. "That can't be a week old," he muttered. "What should we do? Should we go back?"

I was starting to have my doubts.

"No," I finally said. "Of course not. We've got the spray."

After a few minutes of coaxing, Matt agreed to abandon this latest piece of documentary fodder so we could continue up the trail. John resumed his position as leader of our group, although the gap he allowed between himself and the rest of us had narrowed considerably.

A few minutes later, the thing I had put on the bottom of our list made it to the top. It was John, the leader, who made the final confirmation.

"Holy crap!" he yelled back to us, his voice an odd blend of amazement and fear. "A bear. A helluva big one!"

He came running back to get the spray, and we listened to the bear as it crashed off into the woods. Clearly, John and the bear had managed to scare each other.

Matt pointed the video camera into the underbrush beside the trail, but captured nothing more interesting than the faint shaking of a few leaves.

John grabbed the spray from the side of my pack, released the lock, and stood holding it like a gun. "Should I shoot?" he asked, checking with me before he blasted the forest where the bear had crouched a few seconds earlier.

"Hold on a minute!" I barked.

"Yeah, wait!" agreed Matt. "I want to record the spraying on camera."

So there we stood in the middle of the trail, waiting, knowing that a vanishing bear was somewhere in the vicinity. Ten minutes passed and we heard nothing but the sound of our breathing. All the while, questions were spinning through my head. Should we retreat and walk back to the trailhead, or continue to our campsite?

"Let's try it!" John said enthusiastically.

"Try what?" I asked, snapping back to the present.

"The spray. We can check to see if it works. And if the bear is still hanging around, it will clear him out of the area."

Matt immediately agreed. The votes were in and I was in the minority, so John extended his arm, held out the canister of spray, and pressed the button. A powerful jet of orange spray shot out of the can, blanketing ferns, leaves, tree trunks, wildflowers— everything in its path.

"Keep firing! Keep firing!" said Matt, who was getting it all on camera.

Even I was impressed. "Give me that," I finally said. I had to try it for myself.

"And here's Dad," said Matt as he continued filming his documentary. "He's blasting the hell out of the bear. Or is that the forest?"

The three of us stood and watched the mist disperse. A gentle wind carried it away from us, down the slopes and along the trail we had just hiked. We all felt a bit safer and I was quite proud of the massive final blast I had given the defenseless shrubbery.

"Let's wait a few minutes and then we'll carry on," I said. We put our packs down on the trail and took a pleasant break, with cold water and candy bars for everyone—a well-deserved treat after our tense "ordeal."

And then we heard the sound of coughing.

"Is that the bear returning?" asked John.

I listened. "No, that's human coughing. Someone must be having a hard time climbing." We listened more intently. "Sounds like they have a bad cold or something. They're just hacking and hacking."

A group of hikers came around the corner and into view. They were moving slowly, coughing, clearing their throats, and rubbing their eyes. They reached us and then moved past. "There's something weird in the air up here," one of them said.

"Yeah. We smelled it too," I replied.

I waited for the boys to say something, but some odd sense of loyalty kept them silent. John smiled at me. Matt was busy photographing the struggling hikers to gather evidence of the effectiveness and potency of the spray.

"There might be a bear ahead," I offered.

"We'll clear it out for you," the last hiker said as the group disappeared around a corner. In a few seconds, the forest muffled their last faint cough.

Matt and John looked at me, trying to measure what my reaction would be. To be honest, I was filled with embarrassment. I looked at them sternly and told them, rather sharply, that it was no laughing matter. Then I started laughing, and for several minutes none of us could stop.

Finally, John picked up his pack and resumed his position in the lead. "I think it's time we started hiking again," he said.

"Yes," answered Matt. "Let's go. We're invincible!"

And we did. And we were.

Glenn Kletke was born and educated in Manitoba, then moved to Ottawa to pursue a career in teaching. Now retired, he balances his time between writing projects and consulting trips to Singpore and Malaysia. His latest book, House on the Edge of Ice, *is a collection of poems about the vanished Glacier House Hotel in the Selkirk Mountains. He is grateful to his sons for their willingness to spend a decade's worth of summers motoring across Canada to follow their father's infatuation with the Canadian Rockies. He would like to thank the bears from western Canada for sharing their space without offering any major complaints.*

Going Nowhere to See Nothing

There's just something *about that place.*

By Margrit de Graff

After deciding to "get my kicks on Route 66" by riding a bicycle along America's first paved coast-to-coast highway, I began studying a 2001 road map of Arizona. Route 66 and other rambling two-lane highways of its kind have largely been replaced by U.S. interstates—but a small section still remains in the American Southwest.

As I scanned the map, looking for a way to get back to Phoenix after the trip, my eyes traced a line down Route 93 and stopped abruptly at Nothing. A town? A hamlet?

I operate a busy campground in Alberta, Canada, and the season was in full swing, requiring twenty hours of work every day. Yet I could think of nothing but Nothing. I started telling travelers that, come fall, I would visit Arizona to see Nothing. They would usually walk away, no doubt thinking, *Has that woman lost her mind?*

I purchased a new map of Arizona from the Alberta Motor Association and let my eyes wander down Route 93, but I couldn't find Nothing. Was Nothing not there anymore? Alarmed, I dialed an Alberta phone operator to find a number for Nothing, Arizona, hoping to find out something about Nothing.

Rrriiinnnggg. Rrriiinnnggg.

A recorded voice asked, "For what city, please?"

"For Nothing, Arizona."

"For what city, please?"

"NOTHING, Ari—" An operator cut in, asking, "Where are you trying to call?"

"Nothing, Arizona."

"How do you spell that?" she asked.

"N-O-T-H-I-N-G. Can you find me a number for the town's Chamber of Commerce?"

"Ma'am, you have to tell me which city you want to call. I can't help you if you don't tell me where you want to call."

"I'm trying to call someone at the town office or something like that, in a town called NOTHING. It's on Route 93 in Arizona. *It's on the map!*"

Laughter. "You really think there's a town with that name?"

"That's why I'm trying to call there, to find out. It's on a map printed in 2001!"

She paused. "Sorry, ma'am. There's nothing listed under Nothing. I suggest you phone the Chamber of Commerce in Phoenix."

"Thank you, I'll try that."

Rrriiinnnggg. Rrriiinnnggg.

"Good morning. Chamber of Commerce, Phoenix, Arizona. Robert speaking."

"I am calling from Canada."

"Yes?" He didn't sound impressed, likely because his state is crawling with Canadians.

"Can you tell me something about Nothing?"

"Pardon?"

"Can you tell me something about Nothing. I see there is a place in Arizona called Nothing. It's on Route 93."

"Would you spell that for me?"

Here we go again, I thought. "N-O-T-H-I-N-G."

"Nothing ... Nothing?" There was a pause. "You mean like NOTHING?"

"Yes, NOTHING. Is there something in Nothing?"

"Well, never heard of it. There probably *is* nothing there. Maybe you should call Flagstaff."

I hung up. By this time I was feeling *obsessed* with Nothing. I had to find out something about it.

I phoned Flagstaff. A friendly female voice at the Chamber of Commerce answered. After my usual routine, she made the usual request for me to spell NOTHING, which I did.

After a loooonnnggg pause, she asked, "Is it next to nowhere?"

Ha! A sense of humor!

"Well," I said, "On the map I'm looking at, there is nothing next to Nothing. There is a town called Bagdad in the vicinity, but I see no road branching off to Nothing. So yes—as the crow flies, Bagdad would be next to Nothing."

"Give me a minute and I'll ask around the office."

I heard laughter in the background, and a few moments later the woman came back on the line. "Ma'am? There apparently *is* something at Nothing. A gas station, some tow trucks, a store of sorts, and some trailers. It seems Nothing is there, but there's nothing else for miles. Apparently the town is run by a fellow called Old Miner Ben." There was still laughter in her voice.

A few weeks later I traveled to Arizona with my group of cycling friends. As we crossed from Arizona into California on Route 66, I asked our guide what he knew about Nothing.

"Nothing?" he asked. "What is there to know about Nothing? Just some tiny hick town that's miles from nowhere."

"I see."

"If you want to go there, drive south out of Prescott, past Wilhoit, and—let me see—right after Wilhoit comes Nowhere."

"Nowhere? You're kidding!"

"No, I'm not. That's where my wife was born. So you go past Nowhere ..."

I had heard enough. After the bike trip, I decided to rent a car in Prescott and drive through Nowhere until I found Nothing.

A couple of days later I did just that. As I wound through the tall Ponderosa pines, past steep cliffs, and over mountain ranges, the grandiose vistas took my breath away. Driving down from a pass I entered Wilhoit, and shortly thereafter—*Yes!*—Nowhere.

Nowhere sat in a lovely and obviously prosperous valley called the Peeples Valley. There were whitewashed fences, manicured lawns, sprawling ranch houses, and lots of horses. I spent the night at Wickenburg, a historic town on a "wash," as they call the rivers there. At that time of year (October), the rivers and creeks were just ribbons of dry sand.

The next morning I set out searching for Nothing.

After miles and miles of nothing but weird and wonderful

rock formations and cacti big and small, I stopped to photograph a sign that read NOTHING ARIZONA.

I had made it!

I stepped out of my car to look around and my camera clicked happily away. I snapped pictures of a vintage car—1920s era—that was rusted and abandoned. A sign next to a nearby gas station said WATER IS FOR RADIATORS.

I noticed an old fellow watching me from the gas station, so I walked over to say hello. "I've made it!" I said. "I've come a long way to see your town."

"Are you from England?" the man asked.

"No, from Canada."

"Then you didn't come a long way!"

"No? I think that's a very long way to travel to meet you and see your very own town. I noticed it on a map."

"Did you fly?"

"Uh, yes."

"Then you didn't come a long way. It's only two hours from the Canadian border to Phoenix by airplane."

This fellow was one tough customer.

A car stopped. Some pompous-looking guys walked over, and one placed a hand on the old man's shoulder. In a patronizing voice, he asked, "And how is Old Miner Ben today? Made a few bucks yet?" After a pause, he added, "Can we buy candy here?"

"No, I don't sell candy."

"What can we buy here? Come on, we want to spend money on you!"

Old Miner Ben didn't respond. I had a feeling he didn't exactly take a shine to these characters.

The guy put his hand on Miner Ben's shoulder again. "Can we at least get a cup of coffee?"

"Well," said Miner Ben slowly, "you can, but you'll have to wait at least twenty minutes. There is no electricity here. I have to get the radiator going." Then he seemed to change his mind. "Actually, water is reserved for clients with radiator troubles. I have to see how much water is left, but I don't think I can spare some for coffee right—"

But the guys had lost interest by now. They walked back to their car, laughing.

Miner Ben winked at me. "Got rid of them bigwigs." Then, without missing a beat, he asked, "You want a cup of coffee?"

"You don't like their attitude, eh?"

"No, I don't. Them types think they can get anything with the snap of a finger."

I noticed a gas pump at his service station, but it didn't look like it was used much. The front window was opaque with dust. The entrance was blocked by two battered trucks, some old stuffed chairs with the upholstery split open, and a lethargic old dog sprawling on a blanket. As we walked past, the dog didn't even wag his tail when I said hello. A few moments later I was standing among a hodgepodge of items in Miner Ben's little store.

The first thing that struck me was a huge amethyst from Brazil. With a price tag of $1,496.00, it stood in sharp contrast to cheap T-shirts with NOTHING ARIZONA printed on them. There were slices of rock with their beautiful insides revealed, and pieces of petrified wood that sold for $1.50 per pound.

Miner Ben hardly believed me when I told him we had lots of petrified wood near Gull Lake, close to where I lived in Alberta.

"Gull Lake? Never heard of it."

"It's beautiful."

"It has water all the time?"

"Yes, all the time."

He looked thoughtful.

"I drove through Nowhere yesterday," I said, changing the subject. "You know the place?"

"Know the place? Sure do! Them beggars sell everything for a dollar more. *Everything!*"

I looked at his rocks again. After a long, peaceful silence, he said, "Cold country up there in Canada. You better move down here, where it's warm. It's better for you."

I took a few more photos. He seemed pleased at my interest, though few words were spoken. I noticed that the wall was plastered with letters from all over the world, all addressed to Old Miner Ben. There were a lot of photos of different people, usually posing with Ben in front of his store, plus newspaper clippings and other write-ups obviously written by people who were as curious about this unusual place as I was. Did they come here because they found Nothing on a map, or because they just happened by? Whatever the case, that unassuming little old miner drew them in.

"You can take a shortcut back to Nowhere," Miner Ben told me as I prepared to leave. "Take the new road to Bagdad, then turn left when you hit the junction. That will bring you back to Nowhere, and from there you can follow 89 back to Prescott."

I found that road of new, smooth pavement, and drove across a parched moonscape absolutely devoid of vegetation. Not even a cactus! Just a sea of dark boulders retreating in all directions.

I finally reached the tiny town of Hillside, which had two rows of modest bungalows, a tiny school, and a small school bus. As I drove through, I noticed two neighbors talking over a white picket fence. They turned in unison to the stranger, driving past with her windows wide open, and waved. Friendly waves. Then they continued their conversation, unperturbed.

Killing time in a park before my flight home from Phoenix, I struck up a conversation with a fellow who was walking his dog. I told him about Nowhere and Nothing, expecting him to say something like "Huh?" Or, if by chance he'd heard about them, "What godforsaken places!"

"I wish I could live there," he said, to my surprise. "That region is *so* peaceful."

And so it was that I went to Arizona and found something at Nothing. There's no question I'm much better for it.

Margrit de Graff has a knack for biting off more than she can chew. For years she operated a campground near Lacombe, Alberta while raising a large family, and at every opportunity she escaped to travel the world by foot, by bicycle, on skis, or on crutches. Her most recent adventure—as an eighty-year-old—was spending several months on a cargo ship as it sailed around the world.

Kojo's Island

He looked like a laughing Buddha.

By Chris Czajkowski

To understand Jun's story, you have to know something about me, and you have to know something about wwoofing. Wwoof: no, it has nothing to do with dogs, or stereo speakers. And wwoofers are not (it is to be hoped) "people who throw up in the floatplane," as the owner of Tweedsmuir Air at Nimpo Lake calls them.

This reference to floatplanes is significant because that's how most people get to my place. The only other way is to hike for anywhere between fourteen hours and three days, a lot of it over unmarked virgin forest, swamp, and tundra.

Twenty years ago I made my first trip out here, on foot and alone, with the idea of building a cabin. The British Columbia government has laws against people simply heading into the boondocks and squatting, so I had to have a commercial reason. Ecotourism was to be my savior: that was the only thing suited to the high, harsh climate of the region I had chosen. The water was frozen for half the year, and the winds that barreled down the lake from the 12,000-foot spine of the nearby Coast Range were often so severe that all exposed trees leaned sideways.

This was a small thing I had neglected to notice when swept up by the magnificent views, wine-sharp air, and glorious solitude of my first August visit.

Two years and two months later, a day after I had finished screwing down the metal on the roof of my first cabin, the worst recorded windstorm in living memory passed over northern British Columbia. With fear and trembling I huddled in my sleeping bag beneath the thrumming metal (my tent was long gone), terrified that my roof would go and along with it all my dreams. I knew that whatever I planned to do there, if I survived at all, would be forever dictated by that invisible, fickle, and implacable aeolian battering ram. Which is why I called my new home Nuk Tessli; it means West Wind in the Carrier language, and is a reminder of who is boss.

For the first decade I operated alone. It took me three summers to build the first two cabins. The ground was too uneven and rocky for a wheelbarrow, let alone horses (if there had been any closer than 40 kilometers away), and the only machine I had was a chainsaw. I hauled the logs with a come-along and a peavey, and raised them with a block and tackle. The building "leftovers" were used as firewood. My carpentry was crude—my furniture-making father would have turned in his grave—but the buildings were warm and dry inside and stood up to the storms.

After the building waste was consumed in the stoves, I had to find other firewood. I felled dead trees with the chainsaw, bucked them up, rolled the stove-lengths to the waterfront, and split them into manageable sizes. Then I loaded them into my canoe, paddled them home, unloaded, and hauled them up to the woodshed. I used firewood for both cooking and heating, but rarely used more than three cords in a year—the equivalent of about six full-sized pickup truck loads. Still, collecting and preparing it was a monstrously slow job that took weeks.

I also began to brush out a few trails for easier access to the alpine regions, in anticipation of the tourists I hoped would start beating a path to my door. After all, it was only a twenty-minute floatplane ride from Nimpo.

The wilderness surrounding my home evoked superlatives. The cabins stood at 5,000 feet, and sprawling wildflower meadows were only 1,000 feet higher. Nearby mountains peaked at 8,500 feet. A slow trickle of tourists did come, and I guided and cooked where necessary. But with the buildings complete, I had lots of time to explore. Many of my ramblings were in the high country—on foot in the summer and with snowshoes in the winter. Once every four to six weeks I would make the trek to the nearest post office at Nimpo Lake, a journey that might take a day in summer if I was lucky, and usually took three in winter.

I was not at Nuk Tessli all the time. I needed to earn money, so I planted trees in the spring and presented slide shows in the fall to promote both my ecotourism business and the books I had written by then.

By the time I was fifty, I figured the business warranted another cabin. But I no longer had the energy of a decade before. As luck would have it, three young Germans—friends of friends—wanted some wilderness experience. They were tremendous workers; one was skilled as a builder and could already use a chainsaw. Having so much help with that building was a very different experience than my solitary struggles with the first two. So when one of the young Germans said casually one day, "This would make a great wwoofing place," and suggested I apply to be a host, I embraced the idea with open arms. It was a decision that has significantly changed my life.

W.W.O.O.F. is an acronym for Willing Workers On Organic Farms. It's a worldwide operation that connects small-scale farmers with travelers. Opportunities range from harvesting organic rice in Japan to growing kiwi fruit in New Zealand or digging carrots in Lillooet, BC. Not that I have an organic farm. I am lucky if I can grow a crop of radishes at my altitude. But the organizer of WWOOF Canada told me it didn't matter.

And so into my life came a steady stream of usually young (but not always) people of both sexes from Germany, Switzerland, England, Belgium, Canada, Australia, New Zealand, Korea, and Japan. I warn prospective wwoofers that the work is physically hard—a few of the early ones found it more than they bargained for—because life at Nuk Tessli is not exactly like tending a small vegetable plot. Luckily, the majority have flung themselves into the heavy physical labor with great enthusiasm.

Junsuke Ishizu had spent three months in Calgary learning English before he came to me, but Nuk Tessli was his first ever wwoofing experience. He had come well stocked for a month's stay: in the guest cabin to which I had assigned him, and to which I went after the day's tourists had left, were strewn a multitude of clothes and possessions. There was a small, tinny radio with CD player, a dozen throwaway cameras, a tottering pile of Japanese cigarette cartons, and a large bottle of vodka. Alcohol was a big part of his life; he later showed me pictures of his friends, always at parties and always absolutely plastered. Indeed, I found out later that a serious hangover had almost caused him to miss the tourist plane to Nuk Tessli. During his sojourn with me, however, I never once saw him overindulge in alcohol, nor complain about the lack of it.

Clothes-wise he was not so well prepared. His Nikes were not rugged enough for the rocky terrain and swamps he would be expected to work in; his pants were too new; and his crocheted hemp hat was of very loose construction, each hole a perfect conduit for the mosquitoes to reach his freshly shaven head. So I let him rummage in the spare clothes box and he found a complete outfit down to a pair of gargantuan boots that he was forced to stuff with extra socks. The pants he favored were castoffs of mine, relegated to the box after I had put on too much weight. They were so baggy on him that they barely clung to his hips, but he thought they were *really* cool.

Jun's English was not too bad. He spoke rapidly and with confidence, if not with a great deal of precision. Overall, he communicated well. The day he arrived was pristine: a deep blue sky reflected in the lake and soaring snowy mountains rising high to the west. Jun stared at this scene, enraptured.

"Can I swim?" he asked.

"Of course," I replied. "But it's cold."

"Can I ... Can I ... naked?"

"No problem," said I.

Gleefully, he thrust a disposable camera into my hands, flung off his clothes, and waded into the lake. "Take picture for my Mom," he said.

Jun was as green as they come as far as "practical" work went. Most Asian visitors to my wilderness seem to be this way. They live deep within large cities, without the remotest connection to anything natural. Apparently, Jun lived in a suburb with a garden and a dog, but he never helped with the gardening. His mother worked in a bank.

Jun had absolutely no idea of the relationship between his food and the environment. He did not know, for instance, that birds ate berries. He had never canoed. One day I brought along my fishing rod and caught a fish, and when I showed him how to gut and clean it, a caviar of insects spilled out of the stomach cavity. "Fish eat flies?" he squeaked with such alarm that I doubted he would ever eat fish again. (Actually, he said "fries." Like most Asians, he had difficulty with the *l* and *r* sounds.)

Needless to say, his experience with any kind of tool before he came to Nuk Tessli was zero. He clutched his first axe with both hands as if it might fly out of his grip, lifted it a few centimeters, then brought it down with a gentle tap onto a firewood round. He looked quite startled when it bounced up with barely a mark. I gave him a few pointers and left him to it. He struggled for an hour or so, then stuck his head into my cabin. "Enough?" he asked hopefully. But his small bundle of sticks was barely enough to cook a single meal, so back to the woodshed he had to go.

For all of Jun's slim build, he could, like most wwoofers, pack away large quantities of food. When he first arrived I also had to give him a couple of lectures about waste. Nuk Tessli is far from stores; I must shop for the whole summer in May, and if we run out of an item, it's usually difficult to replace. My first complaint, for instance, was the large puddle of maple syrup he left swimming on his plate. I did not mind how much he ate; but waste, I told him firmly, was not to be tolerated.

He learned, of course, just as I learned from him. After he had been with me for a couple of weeks, we were visited by an American who had a summer cabin at Nimpo, and who occasionally dropped by Nuk Tessli in his own plane. He left us with a large melon—an unprecedented treat—so we both hacked off generous slices and tucked in. But Jun left a good inch of flesh on his rind. At once I reminded him of my "no waste" policy.

"Excuse me," he said, "but in my country we have a lot of melons and it is not polite to eat right to the skin. If I did that, they would call me a yucky boy. Is very bad manners."

I apologized, of course, whereupon Jun eyed the half-eaten melon slice and said, "But I am in Canada now." With that, he picked it up and cleaned it off.

Jun's main job at Nuk Tessli was brushing out trails. I wanted to extend the existing trail that ran along the north shore of my lake past the portage, running it along the next lake that was just upstream. For the more distant areas, we worked together. Jun was a novice canoeist who could not swim, so although he learned everything quickly and listened carefully to what I said, I did not want him venturing too far on his own. Once he understood what was expected, he could paddle up the lake to the nearer section, take lunch and cigarettes, and stay there for the rest of the day. It was probably more solitude than he'd ever had in his life, so it can't have been easy for him. But he never complained. Not even on the day he saw the bear.

I have two dogs, both SPCA specials, and both (by coincidence) Rottweiler-colored. Bucky, in particular, has quite a lot of ginger on his legs and head. When Jun came home that night, he said he had heard an animal creeping through the thick brush, apparently trying to sneak around him. By bending down, he had glimpsed the animal's feet. "They were not thin and pointed, like deer," he said. "They were thick with long hair and flat feet. Same color as Bucky's feet. I think it was a bear."

I laughed and told him it most certainly was a bear. "What did you do?" I asked.

"I went back to the canoe. I stayed long enough to smoke two cigarettes. Then I went back to work. But I was frightened. I was singing."

I thought this was both very brave and very sensible of him.

"What language did you sing in?" I asked.

"Japanese" he replied, surprised at my question.

"That's no good," I told him. "It's a *Canadian* bear. It can only understand English."

Canoeing activities in particular are always dictated by *Nuk Tessli*, the West Wind. One morning a gale was blowing. Jun was not naturally an early riser, and considering it was too windy for him to canoe up the lake, I walked over to his cabin to tell him he could stay longer in bed. That was when I discovered something—sleep was not the reason he came late to breakfast. He was meditating. He and his family belonged to a Buddhist sect and every morning, and sometimes in the evening, he spent an hour chanting a mantra. In front of him, on the table, was a little pouch attached to a leather thong. He had been wearing it like a necklace when he arrived.

Jun spoke often of his mother and he was obviously very fond of her. Now he told me of his father, who had died very suddenly just before Jun had come to Canada. It was obvious that Jun was still having a hard time coming to terms with this. He showed me a picture of a chubby man with a large grin, who looked like a laughing Buddha.

"He was a very popular man," said Jun. "Very well respected. One thousand people came to the funeral."

Jun had decided to cancel his Canadian travel plans, but his mother insisted he continue. She had visited him in Calgary, bringing him his stock of strong Japanese cigarettes; he had begged her for them, saying Canadian cigarettes were too weak). She had also brought with her some of her husband's ashes. Jun had deposited little bits in places that he had enjoyed in Canada, and the remainder now lay in the little pouch on the table. He asked me if he could leave them at Nuk Tessli.

"Of course," I said.

His first choice for a site was one of the many peaks that surrounded my lake, but it was already the end of September and the weather was not going to let us get far above the treeline. So he chose one of the islands that form a loose ring about my cabins. From it he could see the peaks he had scrambled up earlier that summer, the area where he had been working, the cabins, and the permanent snows that cover the 12,000-foot giants beyond the head of the lake. It was already windy as he launched the canoe, paddling jerkily across the water. He pulled the canoe on shore and I could hear the waves slapping and bumping it erratically against the stones. The sun was behind him and Jun's slim figure was silhouetted against the sky as he built a small cairn. He then made his farewells, the ragged strains of his chant scattered by the wind.

Jun flew to Nimpo a couple of days later. He hugged me on the wharf, and there were tears in his eyes when he said, "My father's name is Kojo. Speak to him sometimes, will you? Otherwise he will be lonely."

And speak to him I do. Kojo's Island is in front of the lowest point in the horizon as seen from my home, which happens to be the place where the sun rises on the shortest day. As the long, purple shadows of the island's wind-bent trees fan out toward me, I know that the darkest days of winter have passed and spring is on its way. It is an important day for me, for I am very much a creature of the light. And in that small way, Kojo's shrine remains a symbol of hope.

Many wwoofers have come and gone from Nuk Tessli, and all have left their imprint in different ways. But only Jun has left me the spirit of a man who looked like a laughing Buddha, and the memory of the son who mourned him.

Chris Czajkowski lives at Nuk Tessli, a high-altitude fly-in lake near BC's Tweedsmuir Provincial Park, from which she guides artists and naturalists on backpacking trips through BC's Coast Mountains. She is an artist and author of several bestselling books, including Cabin at Singing River *(Camden House, 1991), the story of building her first log cabin 43 kilometers from the nearest road. This story was adapted from her recent book* Wildfire in the Wilderness *(Harbour Publishing, 2006). To learn more about the Nuk Tessli alpine experience, visit Chris at **www.nuktessli.ca**.*

Almost in the Movies

The art of being in the wrong place at the wrong time.

By Russell & Penny Jennings

From beyond the wall in front of us, my wife Penny and I could hear rhythmic drumbeats accompanied by warlike chants. Above the din, a French movie director yelled something to his film crew through a megaphone. The drumbeats thundered louder and faster, and the warlike chants of the Ghanaian film extras rose to a crescendo.

I turned to Penny, who looked hesitant. "I'm not sure we should go ahead," she said.

As it turned out, she was right.

When we had boarded a bus earlier that day in Accra, Ghana's capital, we never imagined we would be in a movie—our destination was simply the coastal fishing village of Elmina. After a three-hour bus ride along a blacktopped road that occasionally hugged the coastline, we arrived at the village, which was dwarfed by a gigantic lime-white castle. The earliest known European building in tropical Africa, the castle was built by the Portuguese in 1482 as a trading post, using rock from the headland on which it stood. It was one of more than fifty castles and forts built by Europeans trading in gold, ivory, and slaves along Ghana's 560-kilometer coastline.

At the time the castle was built, most of Europe's maritime nations were involved in trade with West Africa, and this led to fierce rivalry between them. In 1637, during the slave-trading era, the Dutch captured the castle from the Portuguese. And in 1872, when the business of slavery was beginning to disappear from West Africa, the Dutch sold it to the British, who named it Saint George's Castle.

We arrived to find cars and trucks marked Ghana Films parked outside the castle and a horde of people, mainly black Africans, milling around the castle entrance. *Probably hoping to be extras,* I thought. A skinny blonde French woman with bright red lips appeared from the crowd; she told us a French company was making an historical film and the castle was closed.

I explained that we had come a long way to see the castle and we weren't able to come back another day. As I presented our case, a Frenchman with a shaved head and a ring through his nose approached. He turned out to be the director.

"What's the film about?" I asked him.

He looked nonplussed. "It's the re-enactment of an attack by Ashanti warriors against the Europeans in Elmina Castle. We're filming the battle at the sound stage. If you promise to stay away from that area, I'll let you look around."

We promised him we would stay quiet, keep our heads down, and be discreet.

For the next two hours, we explored the castle's dungeons, storerooms, and battlements. The dungeons that had once housed slaves awaiting shipment to the New World were truly hellish. The only light and ventilation came from a small barred window the size of a ship's porthole, located twenty feet above the ground. An open drainage channel served as the only toilet facility.

We walked in silence and tried to imagine the degradation that had been suffered in this horrific place. There had been no shortage of slaves to be traded as human cargo—conflicts had increased between tribes when they realized prisoners-of-war could be sold for profit at the castles or forts.

From the dungeons, we climbed to the battlements. Cannons faced the open sea, positioned to defend against European ships prowling for plunder. As we continued to explore, we peeked around corners, watching for cameras that might be pointed in our direction. We were being *very* discreet.

When we were ready to leave, a member of the Ghanaian film crew, black as charcoal and wearing dark sunglasses, offered to show us out. He told us to follow him behind the audio crew, down the stairs and off the set.

It seemed like a good plan.

Our guide checked ahead and waved us forward. But we hesitated. From beyond the wall ahead, we could hear rhythmic drumbeats. Whoops and war cries filled the afternoon air, and got louder as the drumming grew more frenetic. We could hear the demanding voice of the French director yelling at his film crew over a megaphone.

Should we be going ahead? Penny didn't think so, nor did I. But the crewmember seemed confident. He turned again and motioned for us to follow him. Did he know what he was doing? I hoped so.

We crept toward the back of the sound stage, barely breathing as we waited for the right moment to cross. Even as the drumbeats and warlike yells grew in intensity, our guide turned to us and loudly whispered, "Now!"

We stepped onto the dark stage and made it halfway across before we heard the film director shout, "Take One!"

The floodlights came on and caught us in their glare. The cameras rolled. We felt as though our feet were nailed to the floor. My heart beat like an Ashanti drum.

At that moment, a hundred or more Ashanti warriors—a mass of bare torsos, loincloths and feathers—stormed the castle compound, waving spears and clubs as they war-danced their way onto the stage to re-enact a battle.

We were mild-mannered, camera-toting travelers from the twentieth century, caught between two warring factions from the 1800s.

From the middle of the melee, up popped the French woman like a champagne cork, frantically waving us back and shaking her fist. As we turned, the director yelled, "Cut!" A barrage of expletives erupted over his megaphone, though I could barely hear what he was shouting above the din of drumbeats. His angry eyes flashed; his hand jerked toward the castle's gate. The message was loud and clear: *Get out.*

I wished I could have evaporated. I repeated "Sorry" and "Excusez-moi" dozens of times as we crossed the stage and scurried past the furious director, the bewildered camera crew, the warriors, the extras, and the hangers-on, making our way none too fast toward the front entrance. The French woman, now wild eyed, tore at her hair with her long red fingernails. Penny and I sprinted for the exit without looking back.

We didn't wait to be called for a second take!

Russell and Penny Jennings connected in 1975 on a blind date. Since then, they have left their sandal prints in dozens of countries on six continents. One such place is India, where they stayed in zero-star hotels as they crisscrossed the country by train and foot. During their three-month odyssey, they gorged themselves on four hundred bananas each. Their home is Vancouver, where they ban bananas from their fruit bowl. Visit the Jennings online at **www.worldweatherguide.com***.*

Moon River

*Note to self: Keep pants on in presence of
police officer.*

By Robert Fulton

"Buy a tripod. You can't take decent pictures without one, especially in a fluid environment like a river. Any landscape photographer worth his salt owns a tripod. And how are you going to get yourself into any pictures without one?"

I enjoy hearing the advice of professional shutterbugs; it reminds me there are still giants among us.

So there I was, standing in my hip boots in three feet of winter-cold river water with my camera securely mounted on my ProPhotographer Signature Model tripod. I was eagerly lining up a "dramatic" shot of some rocks. I shoved the three legs into the gravel and cranked the camera down to within two feet of the flowing surface, then squatted to look through the viewfinder, ensuring the correct upward angle for the picture. Ice water poured down my thighs and into the backs of my boots.

Note to self: Don't squat in hip boots.

By way of some challenging gymnastics I lined up the shot, set the ten-second shutter release, and "raced" into the picture frame. Stepped in a hole. Waist deep. Didn't make it into that picture.

Note to self: Buy a remote-control shutter release.

Emptied the water out of my boots a second time and semi-dried my clothes on the rock. Things weren't going well out here in the river, so I repositioned the camera for a dramatic feeder-stream-waterfall-flowing-into-the-river photograph. Shallower water over there. Going to be much easier, I told myself. Loaded all the gear into my kayak and paddled to the shallows.

Set the three legs of my ProPhotographer Signature Model tripod in the gravel. Aimed the camera at the little waterfall. Carefully bent over at the waist to peek through the viewfinder … and dunked the camera bag hanging around my neck into the water. Extra film, my camera's operating manual, and a half-eaten pack of Cheetos all blended into a soggy morass at the bottom of the bag.

Note to self: Leave camera bag in the kayak.

The kayak!

I had been so distracted emptying my camera bag and spreading its orange-tinted contents on a nearby rock that I momentarily forgot about my boat. Yep, there it was, languidly drifting downstream, its progress occasionally hampered by a protruding rock. I took off after it, taking the river with me, half in each boot. Got absolutely soaked sloshing down with the current.

Note to self: Secure watercraft when not aboard. Purchase chest waders.

By the time I collected my ProPhotographer Signature Model tripod and camera bag with its mushy contents, emptied water out of my boots for a third time, and paddled back to the truck, I was turning blue and shivering uncontrollably. The landing was well below the river bridge, so I stripped off my wet clothes before hypothermia could set in.

"Sir, why are you stripping at a public boat ramp?" The voice came from behind me. I turned around and came face to face with a police officer.

"Deputy, I'm f-f-freezing and I have to get some dry clothes on."

"Have you been drinking, sir?"

"What? No I haven't b-b-been drinking. I was trying to take photographs of the r-r-river rocks and waterfall."

"Sir, we've had two cellphone calls from motorists who've seen a drunk splashing around in the middle of the river."

"May I get d-d-dressed, deputy?"

I grabbed a stained sweatshirt from behind the truck seat. It smelled like motor oil, but it was dry. No pants, but I did have a black trash bag I'd kept to collect the debris that careless people leave around boat ramps. I tore holes in the bottom corners of the bag and stuck my feet through. Tied the yellow drawstring around my waist and was ready to ride. I heard a car door shut and watched a hatless and laughing deputy wipe tears from his eyes as he drove off.

Note to self: Law enforcement should be serious business!

The trip back was going fine until I had to use the bathroom. Pulled into a Burger King, swished inside, and noticed friendly conversation grind to a halt. Patrons stopped talking and stared at me ... but nobody said a word. The two fellows in the restroom left in a big hurry. Heck with them!

May as well get something to eat, I thought.

Note to self: Use drive-through when wearing trash bag.

Robert Fulton grew up in south Florida where he fished, camped, and roamed expanses of the Everglades and what is now the Big Cypress Preserve. He regularly contributes to magazines such as Florida Outdoors *magazine and* North Carolina Sportsman, *and is the author of* Swamp Drifter, *a collection of "nature tales, photographs, reminiscences, and rants" about the Great Outdoors.*

French Lessons

Beauty is a serious business in France.

By Colleen Friesen

"*Très, très, très, très bon,*" said the freshly coiffed woman at the *boulangerie* counter. Her oh-so-French manicured nails gleamed as her fingers reached for my chosen baguette. Apparently, I had picked one of her favorites.

Forget what people say about the French and their snobbery. In a month-long driving trip through France, my husband and I were treated like *bons amis*. Admittedly, I did feel like the bumpkin-esque friend, the poor girl with an obvious lack of fashion sense. But still, the French were kind, in the way that clearly superior people can be, as they indulged our charmless existence.

We were armed with only a rental car, a guidebook, the French we had gleaned from Corn Flakes boxes *(Flocons de Maïs!)* and precision Michelin maps. We had no problems wherever we went.

Well, almost none.

Michelin maps are great, but even with their incredible detail, there will be—let us call them—*moments*. It has been said that the true test of a marriage is wallpapering together. *Au contraire.* It is driving in France with Kevin as the driver and myself in charge of the maps.

After some rather animated discussions, I came to believe that life would ultimately be improved if it were more like a French road. Kevin and I soon learned that mistakes really didn't matter. In mere moments there would be another *rond-point* where there would be at least four more chances to drive in a different direction. These roundabouts were the ultimate redemption. Didn't like Road A? Drive to the next circle until you find the name of the town you want to visit, and you can twirl your little car into an entirely new direction. Life's choices should be so easily corrected.

It's not just the French roads that illustrate a different approach to life. It's the way the French pride themselves in living their lives as art. They dress, for instance, as if it actually matters. The French recognize that baggy sweat pants and running shoes with inflated tongues are not casual dress clothing options. They have a phrase, *la chose bien faite*—the thing well made, the thing well done, or the life well lived.

And so I found myself in a land of women with flawless brows and precision-lined lips, each one of them, young and old, exuding allure. Forget talk about the slow-food movement; these people have perfected the *slow-life* movement. Quite clearly, all this preening takes time. Life, as it's been said, is in the details.

Living well is an art, and art doesn't end with grooming. City after town after village, no matter the size, we found common themes: a bakery with only the freshest of breads; a *pâtisserie* with fairytale confections; and a butcher with a variety of meats that inspired dreams of chef lessons. Naturally, there is also the produce shop. The perfectly ripe peach with the green leaf still clinging to its stem will await purchase next to the basket of zucchini flowers. And of course, a town of any size will have an entire store dedicated to chocolate. As it should be.

Given such culinary perfection, it makes perfect sense to take two-hour lunches and to drink wine at every meal. Except breakfast—though we saw that too.

Every region has its specialties. More often than not, our huge Michelin chart read like a menu instead of a map. In Dijon each restaurant table has a pot of *moutarde* beside the salt and pepper. In Chamonix we gorged on fondue *Savoyarde*; in Roussillon we ate the wonderful *cassoulet*; and on the Rhone we ate *Valrhona* chocolate.

When we arrived in Vichy, I decided it was time for the full spa treatment. I left Kevin to park the car while I went seeking Vichy's famous *eau*. When I pictured myself "taking the waters," I envisioned low lights, scented oils, and me ... languid and relaxed. By now I had a hidden hope, a wish for more than just a world-class spa treatment. I wanted something else to happen. Something French.

Maybe this *séance* would gain me entry into this hidden world of divinely elegant women. Perhaps my *thérapie* would let me in on the seemingly unfathomable beauty secrets of my French sisters. Was it just perfect posture that made them so chic as they perched on café chairs sipping espressos from Barbie-doll cups? I, too, wanted to be the kind of woman who entices a scarf to float, cloud-like, around her neck. Surely after a four-handed massage treatment I would be transformed. I would share their aura of that certain *je ne sais quoi*. I saw myself emerging, elegant and poised, with a glowing *visage*.

Moments later, I am still clinging desperately to that thought as I grip the stainless steel handrail next to the white-tiled wall. I am buck-naked and standing in a brightly lit room that resembles a small operating theatre. A petite woman in a crisp lab coat is pressure-washing me with a hose that would work well for crowd control.

The water blasts off the coarse sea salts that are crusting my skin. Before this, four strong hands had given new meaning to "exfoliation." I was quite sure my epidermis had been sanded off with their rubbing—but I was wrong. The *fire hose* is doing that.

The woman mimes the next position: I am to turn and lift my arms, one after the other. She emphasizes that I should always keep my other hand firmly on the bar. *Bien sûr.* Then she sweetly points the jet and blasts more therapeutic Vichy water at my armpits. I make a silent vow never to pressure-wash my deck again.

Finally, she's done. As am I.

The hose falls heavily to the tiles. The other woman in a hospital coat takes me by the elbow and guides me, trembling, to the changing area. With her minimal English and my rather useless French, I understand that I am to dry myself off. I begin preparing to leave.

"*Mais non*," she says, and leads me back to the table. There's fresh plastic laid down. Apparently we're not done. I'm beginning to understand why they call it a beauty regime.

I lie on my mottled red back. She places a bucket between my ankles. "*Masque*," she says, holding a gooey handful of black mud up to my face for verification. Starting at my toes, twenty French fingers knead, smear, and rub this magic muck into every joint. My belly is kneaded and squeezed like defiant dough. I feel the mud heating up as they slather more and more into my muscles. It's creamy, but thick and slightly resistant to their pushing.

Reaching my hairline, they stop and ask me to turn over. I slide my slimy body into position, laying my face on a fresh towel. More muck. More massaging. And then the four-nozzled shower bar I had seen earlier is swung into position over the table. A monsoon of Vichy water cascades onto my tenderized body. Fingers slip and sluice the muddy water off my tingling skin. I realize that I am moaning into my towel. I can't stop, I feel so good. I'm quite sure this can't be legal.

Stunned, I re-enter the outside world. I blink and almost stumble as I step onto the sidewalk, and then I remember ... I'm in on *the secret*.

I arrange my big sunglasses on my glowing face and walk, sure-footed, toward the shops. I'm buying a scarf.

Life is *très, très* bon.

Colleen Friesen never intended to be a writer, but after entering a travel essay contest and winning an umbrella, she was hooked. When she found out that people would actually pay her to travel, her fate was sealed and she's barely been without a boarding pass since. Rejection and editorial criticism pales in comparison to her previous life as the only female log broker in British Columbia's wild and woolly forest industry. She lives on the Sunshine Coast with her husband Kevin Redl.

The Voice of Peace

Being a disc jockey on the world's most unique pirate radio station.

By David Litvak

The *Voice of Peace* was a legendary pirate radio station that at one time broadcast from "somewhere in the Mediterranean"—an old Dutch cargo ship off the coast of Tel Aviv, Israel.

Funds to purchase the ship and its broadcasting equipment were raised by Abie Nathan, the famous Jewish peace activist from Iran, shortly after he made a daring solo biplane flight to Egypt to deliver a message of peace to Egyptian President Gamal Abdul Nasser. Nathan was arrested and sent back to Israel, where he established the VOP in 1973 to promote peace and dialogue between Israelis and Arabs.

Before coming to Israel, I had been a graduate student at the University of Manitoba and a disc jockey at a hard-rock bar in my Canadian hometown of Winnipeg. But while I was living in Ottawa, conducting research for a Master's thesis on broadcasting, I met a fellow grad student who told me about the pirate radio station anchored off the Israeli coast. I was intrigued. The idea of being a deejay on a pirate radio ship that promoted peace through music sounded like a grand adventure—not to mention the ultimate broadcasting experience for a formerly landlocked prairie dweller.

So it was that after a fabulous year of working, traveling, and studying in Israel, I applied to work on the *Voice of Peace* during the winter of 1991. I got the job, and it wasn't long after that I hopped aboard a speedboat from a dock in Tel Aviv and was whisked five kilometers through choppy waters to the peace ship.

During its heyday in the 1970s, the VOP had up to twenty million listeners in Israel, Turkey, and Southern Europe. It sailed to Cyprus, and twice each to Egypt and Lebanon, on missions of peace and goodwill. By the time I joined the peace vessel, however, it felt more like a ghost ship than a world famous pirate radio station. The skeleton crew consisted of a captain and first mate from the Philippines, a cook from India, a deckhand and several disc jockeys from the United Kingdom, and me, the token Canadian.

Not long after I joined the peace ship, some of the British disc jockeys were preparing to resign because of the stormy weather at sea, and they advised me to do the same. I decided to ignore their advice and make the best of this once-in-a-lifetime opportunity. As the waves hurled against the ship broadside, rocking it back and forth, I often found myself struggling to retain my balance and my last meal. I kept reminding myself that this was a character-building experience. And besides, whenever I got into the studio, it was all worth it.

The vessel had been transformed into a floating radio station by adding a transmitter, a music library, and production studios. I honed my radio chops on a variety of shows ranging from *Twilight*

Time, The Peace Program, Modern Rock, and *All Time Number Ones* to the classical and country music programs. I found music for my programs in the ship's extensive library, where I spent countless hours browsing through the stacks of records. To my surprise, there were dozens of Canadian albums. Whenever I could I would slip in music from Bryan Adams, Gordon Lightfoot, Neil Young, and Blue Rodeo—which may have confused our Middle Eastern listeners. As far as I know, however, there were never any complaints.

When the seas were calm, broadcasting from the VOP's studios was no different than broadcasting from a conventional radio station. But when the seas were rough on the Mediterranean, *everything* aboard the VOP was rocking and rolling. Including me. And if I happened to be on air at the time, it made broadcasting a lot more challenging. Not only would I slide back and forth across the studio, hanging on to the microphone for dear life, but CDs would often fly off the shelves and hit me in the head. Rough seas often caused our CDS to skip and made cueing up records on our turntables a *lot* more challenging. But admittedly, these unique aspects of broadcasting aboard the *Voice of Peace* were also part of the fun.

On several occasions, while lounging on the deck of the VOP and gazing at the azure waters of the Mediterranean, I spotted schools of dolphins swimming by. Another time, an Israeli naval gunboat cruised past and the sailors yelled out song requests. What could we do? We played them.

When the *Voice of Peace* sailed to the Israeli ports of Haifa and Ashdod to replenish our fuel and water supplies, the deejays on board were even recruited to help the ship dock. It made us feel like bona fide sailors. And on Saturday afternoons when the seas were calm, Israelis would excitedly wave at us as they cruised past in their sailboats and yachts. It was moments like these that we felt like celebrities.

Life aboard the ship was far from glamorous, however. I remember one occasion when I had to help my friend Nick—a deckhand from Manchester who referred to me as a "Canippy" (Canadian Hippy)—guide and unravel the ship's anchor chain. It was a dirty and disgusting job. At other times, deejays would be recruited for the dangerous job of climbing the station's transmitter, which was located on the top deck—a task I never volunteered for.

And then there were the storms—so many, in fact, that I began to lose track. For the most part they were an inconvenience; they made everyday tasks like eating, walking, or going to the bathroom more challenging. (For example, while eating, our plates would slide back and forth across the table.) But during one hair-raising storm, the worst we experienced while I was on the *Voice of Peace*, we almost had to abandon ship.

In the middle of a pitch-black night, gigantic waves slammed relentlessly against the side of the ship. From below deck we could hear the anchor chain being dragged across the ocean floor—an eerie sound. When the storm began, I was watching a video with some of the other deejays, though it wasn't long before the crashing of the waves caught our attention. We raced to the top deck to see what was happening, and found the crew frantically scrambling to prepare the life rafts in case we had to abandon ship.

As we stood there shivering in the wind, we witnessed a surreal sight: the *Arutz Sheva*, another Israeli pirate broadcasting vessel, floated by us with a snapped anchor chain. It looked like the Flying Dutchman. No sooner did it appear than it was swallowed again by the darkness. Fortunately for us, the storm eventually subsided, and both the *Arutz Sheva* and the *Voice of Peace* survived to broadcast another day.

At the end of March, after three months aboard the *Voice of Peace*, I returned to the mainland and spent a few more months studying in Israel before traveling through Europe on my way back to Canada.

On November 28, 1993, a few years after my tour of duty on the *Voice of Peace*, Abie Nathan scuttled his ship in international waters. The Oslo Accords had just been signed, marking the first direct, face-to-face agreement between Israel and the Palestinians; Nathan believed the VOP had fulfilled its mission. With that final act, the swashbuckling station that gave countless neophyte disc jockeys like myself a once-in-a-lifetime broadcasting adventure, now sits at the bottom of the ocean floor somewhere in the Mediterranean.

May it rest in peace.

David Litvak is a prairie refugee from landlocked Winnipeg who now lives in Vancouver, British Columbia. He is a freelance writer and the principal publicist with Cascadia Publicity. His articles have appeared in The Globe and Mail, The Seattle Post Intelligencer, *and* The Forward.

Confessions of a First-Time Gas Siphoner

It sounded like a good idea at the time.

By Matt Jackson

Even in these times of grossly inflated fuel prices, I never thought I would stoop so low as to try siphoning gasoline. I guess one shouldn't underestimate the lengths a desperate man will go to in order to save a few dollars.

Of course, there are always reasons behind every act of stupidity. And for you to understand these reasons, dear reader, it's only fair that I start at the beginning.

It was while driving back to my home in Vancouver, BC— after spending two weeks on a rafting trip in Canada's Northwest Territories—that my faithful station wagon and traveling companion of ten years died. I had just filled her up at a gas station in Prince George when she started vibrating violently and making a sound like she was passing a cat through her carburetor. Even for someone like me, who's not mechanically inclined, it was obvious something was amiss. So I quickly cut the engine.

The cataclysmic noise had attracted a fair bit of attention from other travelers filling their tanks, from the gas station attendant, and from a pair of astronauts onboard an orbiting space station.

An intrigued mechanic from a nearby automotive repair shop sauntered over as I propped the hood up, trying to make it look like I had things under control. It didn't take the mechanic long to offer a diagnosis: one of the cylinders had likely been damaged—a condition that, if true, would prove fatal to the engine.

The next morning they ran a compression test and confirmed the diagnosis, which meant I would either have to buy a new engine for the car or purchase another vehicle. My fiancée and I had moved from Calgary to Vancouver four months earlier, and the thought of another large expense so soon was not heartening.

A twelve-hour Greyhound trip back to Vancouver was my time to grieve—after all, my station wagon and I had been all over North America together. We were pals. We were buddies. It would be like losing an old friend. I decided right then and there that I would do whatever it took to get her back on the road again.

The repair shop called two days later with the damage report: putting a certified rebuilt engine into the old car would cost more than six thousand dollars. I decided that maybe the old wagon and I weren't such good friends after all, and I began searching the online auto trader for another vehicle. I soon found one—two years newer and with only forty thousand kilometres on the odometer— for only $6,700.

The deal was sealed. I would have to send my old friend to the scrapyard.

With my decision made, there was still the challenge of coming up with the necessary funds for the new vehicle. And there always seem to be plenty of annoying "hidden" costs that a person has to absorb when they buy a new car: Goods and Services Tax, Provincial Sales Tax, a vehicle inspection fee, a car transfer fee, a fee to change insurance documents, and the cost of new plates. There was also the ninety-dollar ticket I received for parking in the alley behind our apartment ... because our *damn* garage door opener was still in the glove compartment of the old vehicle! And, of course, there was the cost of the twenty-hour round trip back to Prince George in the new car to pick up my belongings, pay the mechanic's bill, and arrange for my former vehicle to get towed to the auto wreckers.

Perhaps that's why I began to scheme.

I called the auto wreckers as soon as I arrived in Prince George, and they agreed to pay for the towing bill. But they weren't going to give me anything more for the old car. That being the case, I decided to strip a few things from her before handing her over. Things like the floor mats, the factory tape deck ... the wheels. My budget-savvy fiancée was going to be proud of me. Heck, I was proud of myself. I was going to squeeze every possible nickel out of the old girl before I left her for dead.

As I prepared to leave the auto wreckers, I remembered that she also had a full tank of gasoline. I checked the gas gauge on my new car and realized it was almost empty. *There's no reason to waste forty dollars*, I thought. *I may as well take the gas, too.* When I told the scrapyard manager my plans, however, he seemed a bit skeptical. With obvious misgivings, he scrounged a piece of rubber hose and gave it to me.

I unscrewed the gas cap on my old wagon and carefully slid one end of the hose deep inside her tank. I blew into the hose a couple of times to reassure myself that the tank was full. Then I wrapped my lips tightly around my end of the hose, and ever so gingerly, began sucking.

Nothing happened.

I tried again. Still nothing.

I nervously massaged the rubber and inhaled again, this time a little more deeply. When I felt gasoline starting to ascend the hose, I yanked my mouth away. A few drops of gas trickled out the end, but before I could shove it into my new vehicle's gas tank, the trickle had stopped.

Now I had to wipe the hose clean, so I walked inside and asked the attendant for a rag. He shot me a worried look and handed me one from behind the counter.

"Don't worry," I said. "This is going to work."

I returned to my task, repeating almost exactly what I had done before: two shallow drags to work up my nerve, followed by a slightly deeper one that brought a few drops of petroleum dribbling out the end of the hose. For the next five minutes I experimented with different patterns of sucking, realizing for the first time that siphoning gasoline was probably not as easy as the Dukes of Hazzard made it look on television.

On attempt number fourteen (roughly), I could feel the gasoline starting to flow up the hose, so I inhaled powerfully one last time...

... and was treated to a sensation like I've never experienced before.

With that last powerful drag, gasoline hit me like a tidal wave. It went down my throat, up my nose, and from there, directly into my frontal lobe. The sensation was similar to the kind of jabbing pain one feels after eating ice cream too quickly, only longer-lasting and ten times more painful. (For a realistic simulation of how this *feels*, remove the shocks from your car and drive at top speed through a parking lot full of speed bumps while playing Michael Bolton at a high volume.)

After spending fifteen minutes in the auto wrecker's washroom, hunched miserably over the sink and alternately drinking and spitting out water, I emerged into the daylight and handed over the old wagon's keys for the last time. As I left, the manager shot me an "I told you so" kind of look.

Before leaving town, I decided to visit the Prince George hospital. I had no idea how toxic gasoline was, and I didn't like the thought of passing out and pitching off the road in my newly purchased car. The nurses at the emergency ward were very kind, and after calling the poison control center, they ran me through a series of tests.

"I just hope it was Premium," said one nurse, trying not to laugh. Over the next two days, I had the worst case of "gas" I've ever had—every belch flavoured with petroleum.

In a strange twist of fate, my short hospital visit ended up costing me almost two hundred dollars. It turns out that my

Alberta health insurance had expired, and my wife and I had been so busy traveling since moving to BC that we hadn't yet filled out the forms to get our new provincial health cards.

And that, dear readers, is the most expensive tank of gasoline I ever hope to pay for.

Matt Jackson is the president of Summit Studios and author of the award-winning book The Canada Chronicles: A Four-year Hitchhiking Odyssey. *He claims that he would rather slam his fingers in a door, bungee jump naked, or spend an entire day locked in a room with Michael Bolton music playing than taste another petroleum cocktail.*

A Very Persistent Bear

It's all about knowing your adversary.

By Carolyn Kohler

Just when you think you know everything about traveling through bear country, there's a bear that makes you realize how very little you really know. On a recent backpacking trip, we came face to face with such a bear.

My husband Tom and I had backpacked many times in the Ansel Adams Wilderness of California. It is a stunning area filled with sharp-tipped, glaciated peaks and clear blue lakes, and one of our favorite backpacking destinations. For this trip we had invited two close friends, Lisa and Adriane, also avid backpackers, and Tom's city-wise fourteen-year-old nephew, Jake, who hailed from central (and very flat) Indiana. This would be Jake's second backpacking trip, and my husband wanted him to have a great experience in the mountains.

As we put on our packs for the fifteen-kilometer trek, we talked excitedly about the beautiful, untarnished country we were about to enter. We were headed for Thousand Island Lake for four days, and since we would be camping at an elevation of 9,200 feet, we expected to see some snow.

Two miles into our hike, we met up with a weary-looking father and son coming down the trail. "If you are going to Thousand Island Lake, watch out for the bear," they warned. "It got all of our food." We listened to their tale of woe in earnest and offered some of our energy bars to help them get back to the trailhead.

Not long after, we came upon a young man and woman trudging down the trail, so we stopped to exchange information. Their warning echoed that of the first campers we had met: "Be careful of the bear at Thousand Island Lake. It stole our food last night."

We talked briefly about the bear, but decided to carry on. Tom, Lisa, Adriane and I had already made dozens of backpacking trips into bear country. We had pitted our food storage skills against some of the smartest bears in California, and the only incident we'd had was with the infamous car-door-ripping bears of Yosemite Valley. That occasion had made us strict practitioners of the art of proper food hanging—packing one's food in a special bag and suspending it from a high rope strung between two trees, well out of the reach of bears. Since then, we had always managed to keep our food safe. So in spite of the sad stories we had just heard, we felt confident that we would be able to outwit this big, bad bear.

As we headed deeper into the wilderness we started to see snow on the ground—much more than we had expected. So much snow, in fact, we could barely find the trail. When we finally reached Thousand Island Lake, not only was there a lot of snow, but the lake was almost completely covered with ice. "No wonder the bear is stealing food," Lisa said. "It woke up hungry from its winter nap and found this."

We walked along the lakeshore and soon found the perfect campsite. It was a level area with a great view of the lake, and it had a tall tree with high branches strong enough to hang our food from. We set up our tents, with Tom and me in one tent, Lisa and Adrian in a second, and Jake in a third. Tents assembled, we gathered some firewood, made a fire, and then settled in to have dinner. Later, we carefully stowed our food by packing it into two large bags, tying the bags together with a rope, and counterbalancing the rope-tied bags across a limb in our tree. We pushed the bags high up into the tree with a stick, certain that they were well beyond the reach of any bear.

As darkness fell, I walked to the lake for a moment of wonderful silence. I looked around the shore and saw no other campfires. *Hmmm*, I thought. *If there is a bear at the lake tonight, it's going to come looking for us.*

Back at camp, I quietly shared that thought with my husband, feeling that there was no need to alarm Jake.

For those of you who are not familiar with California black bears, they are nocturnal creatures that do not like confrontation. Although they might try to steal your food, loud noises and a few well-aimed stones can usually discourage them. Nevertheless, before turning in, I positioned some pots and pans outside our tent flap. They would act as an early warning system in case a snooping bear attempted to poke his head inside our tent.

Everyone was tired after our long hike, and we quickly fell asleep.

Less than an hour later, I was awakened by a noise like the squeaking of a pulled rope. I grabbed my flashlight and poked my head out of the tent. There was a bear not more than thirty feet away, and since I was lying down and looking up, it looked as large as an elephant. Worst of all, it was holding one of our bags of food in its claws and contentedly chomping away.

"The bear has our food!" I shrieked.

In seconds everybody was awake; you've probably never seen a commotion more comical than five people struggling to get out of their sleeping bags all at once. After crawling out of our tents we yelled at the bear, banged pans together, waved our arms, and threw stones. Finally the bear had enough of our food (and of us) and lumbered away into the darkness.

We quickly assessed the situation. One bag of food had been pulled from the limb onto the ground and was badly mangled. The second bag was still tied to the other end of the rope and was high in the tree, untouched.

"How did the bear ever reach the food bag?" I asked. It had to be one very large bear!

We hung our remaining food, this time forming a human pyramid and using a very long stick to hoist the bag even higher. Unless the bear was fifteen feet tall, it would never be able to reach our food. Or so we thought.

We prepared to retire again, but Jake looked worried. "Come sleep in our tent," my husband suggested. Jake looked relieved.

I was relieved too, since now I would be positioned between two warm bodies and that much harder to get at if the bear felt so inclined.

An hour passed, and I was awakened again by a new noise. This time it sounded like scratching and scraping. I grabbed my flashlight and poked my head outside the tent. The bear was back, and it was climbing our tree. There are few sights as funny as a very large and ungraceful bear trying to scamper up a tree. I woke my husband and Jake, and we howled with laughter as we watched.

It took a few minutes, but the bear finally made it to the limb that held our food. Then it crawled, ever so carefully, across the very small and precarious limb to the rope that held our bag of food. To our astonishment, it then began hoisting one of the food bags, paw over paw, as if it had hands! In a few seconds, the bear had the bag in its jaws.

By that time we were all out of our sleeping bags, yelling and screaming at the bear. It looked down at us placidly and began munching away.

Seeing that the rope was still tied to the bag and was now hanging low enough to the ground for us to reach it, my friend Lisa decided to engage the bear in a tug-of-war. Lisa is not a fragile flower; at five feet ten inches, she can (and regularly does) bench-press a hundred and forty pounds. Lisa grabbed the rope and began to tug. The bear dug in its claws and tugged back.

Lisa tugged harder. The bear hung on. Finally the rope broke and Lisa fell on her backside. Ah well; it had been a noble effort.

We yelled louder, but the bear continued to eat our food. After a few moments, Adrian decided to capture the moment and ran into his tent for his camera. He began snapping photos and we discovered that the bear did not like the bright flash—it let go of the food bag and slowly backed down the tree.

An uneasy moment ensued for all of us. Now that we had tormented the bear from its perch, what would it do? We backed slowly away from the tree, hoping for the best. It seemed to take forever, but the bear finally reached the ground and ran off into the darkness.

Whatever food we had left was now stuck in the tree, and we had no way of reaching it. We decided to go to bed and figure it all out in the morning.

You may have guessed what happened next: the bear came back once again and began clambering up the tree. It must have been just as tired of fighting with us as we were of fighting with it, because a single flashlight in its face made it reconsider. It ran into the woods and didn't come back.

The next morning we awoke tired and hungry, and stared longingly at the bag of food stuck high in the tree. Tom came up with a possible solution: throw a rope over the limb and use it like floss to free the bag of food. With Tom on one end of a rope and Adrian on the other, they worked at the bag of food until it finally fell from the tree.

We looked through the bag to see what was left. This bear must have had a sweet tooth, because all our cookies were gone, along with our hot chocolate mix and our peppermint schnapps. Not only was it a persistent, well-fed bear; it was a drunkard.

After taking an inventory, we figured we had enough untouched food (just barely) to last one more day. We decided to move to a different campsite with no snow and no hungry bears. But as we packed up our gear, we found one more surprise.

The previous night, all of us had leaned our backpacks against a large log five feet from our tent. At some point during the night, the bear had searched our empty backpacks for food, leaving footprints and a telltale trail of saliva. Not one of us had heard a sound. The thought of such a big bear coming so close to our tent gave me goosebumps.

For recent backpacking trips, we've ditched the counter-weighted food-hanging method in favor of a bear-proof PVC canister. We have not had our food stolen since. As for our nephew, he returned to Indiana with a great story about his "ferocious bear encounter," bringing the mangled food bags with him as evidence. It must have been a positive experience for him, since he now lives in the Rocky Mountains of Colorado.

*Carolyn Kohler is a freelance travel writer and photographer. She and her husband Tom Patterman are currently traveling around North America in search of incredible hikes. Carolyn can be reached at **carolyn@carolynkohler.com**.*

Hitch 50

*Or how two clean-cut Canadian university grads
ended up rummaging loose change out of a
stolen car in Kentucky.*

By Matt Fidler

After graduating from university, my friend Scotty and I had no
idea what we wanted to do, at least in the long term. In the short
term, we knew that we wanted to saddle up in my burgundy Dodge
Caravan—which was nearly as old as we were—and drive halfway
across Canada to drink the beer in Scotty's brother's fridge.

Kyle, the aforementioned brother, had recently acquired
a house in a small Saskatchewan prairie town, not far from the
North Dakota border. He was holding Saskatchewan's Biggest
Housewarming Party Ever on the Labor Day weekend, and he had
promised us free beer if we made it through the twenty-two hour
drive from Vancouver Island on Canada's west coast to his new
house on the Prairies. We finished our university program together
on Thursday; our rental lease ran out on Friday. We pretty much
had to go.

What we hadn't determined was our plans *after* that weekend.
We had nowhere to live, nowhere to go, no jobs, and no money. Oh
yeah … and we were headed for rural Saskatchewan. This left us

at Kyle's mercy. As fate would have it, Kyle just happens to be a world champion at coming up with ridiculous ideas; his most recent idea was to trade a red paperclip for increasingly valuable objects until he owned a house. A house in Saskatchewan, to be exact. He now holds a place in Guinness World Records for coming up with ridiculous ideas ... but that's another story.

At the height of the weekend's ceremonies, Kyle had taken the stage and proposed to his French-Canadian girlfriend Dominique. She said "Oui." He had a new house. He had a contract to write a book. Kyle was pretty busy. Nevertheless, all his new commitments didn't stop him from coming up with outrageous ideas, though they did cut into his time to act on them.

Scotty and I couldn't avoid it—we were easy prey for one of Kyle's schemes.

One thing led to another and we soon found ourselves on a train to New York City, where we would start our own ridiculous journey. Kyle had bet us that we couldn't hitchhike to all fifty American states—fifty state capitols, actually—in fifty days or less. Yes, fifty *consecutive* days.

We knew this would probably be impossible using the traditional thumb-on-the-side-of-the-road method alone, so we spent our last few weeks in Saskatchewan building a web site that would track our progress on the trip and promote it to various media outlets. To our surprise, we were doing radio interviews all over America before we'd even started. We proudly told thousands of listeners that we were going to all fifty states in fifty days. Now we really had to go through with this, or we'd be *liars*. And we didn't want to be liars. This taught us a valuable lesson: *Sometimes you have to rummage through a stolen car in rural Kentucky for loose change so that you won't be a liar.*

*   *   *

At the midpoint of our trip, we were on schedule to meet our goal. We had visited twenty-five state capitols in twenty-two days. Things were looking pretty good. We had been interviewed by CNN, MSNBC, USA Today, and dozens of other media outlets. Five thousand people per day were visiting our web site to see where we were and what we were doing.

We were two clean-cut Canadian university graduates, and we were high-tech. Our web site even had a real-time GPS map so people could follow our progress and see exactly where we were at any given moment. That was our edge.

But there were two questions that nagged at us every day— two BIG questions that people always asked us.

1.   How are you going to hitchhike to Hawaii?
2.   How are you going to hitchhike to Alaska?

Both questions were valid. We had no idea. Our approach was blind optimism. All we could do was keep on trucking to all the other state capitols and hope that those two pesky ones just worked themselves out.

One Monday evening in October, we were taking a break from the open road to watch one of the biggest football games of the year: the Southeast Kentucky Middle School Championship game. That's where our last ride had been heading, so that's where we ended up. He had mentioned free burgers, so it wasn't that difficult to convince us.

The game we were watching featured the hometown North Laurel Jaguars taking on the visiting Clay County Raiders. Almost every single one of the teenagers playing was bigger, stronger, and faster then I am now. The stands were packed with diehard fans wearing team jerseys and face paint. That night, in the town of London, Kentucky, this game was the center of the known universe.

Our cellphone rang. There was a good chance the person calling us had something other than the Big Game on their mind, but Scotty answered it anyway.

"Hello?"

"Is this Scotty and Fiddy?"

"Yeah, this is Scotty. Who's this?"

"My name is Josh. On Wednesday, my buddy Trevor and I are flying our new Cessna from Seattle up to Juneau, Alaska. We have some extra seats if you guys want to tag along. I was just wondering if you would to be able to make it."

Those last few sentences hit Scotty like an eighth-grade linebacker. He could barely believe what he had just heard.

"Wow. That's an amazing offer—the only problem is we're in Kentucky right now, so it's going to be a little tough to get to Seattle that fast."

"Yeah, I know. I checked out your site today. But I thought I'd let you know the offer still stands if you can figure out a way to get here in time. You guys always seem to have something up your sleeve."

"Well," said Scotty, "I guess we'll have to find a way to make it."

"I hope you do! We fly out around midday on Wednesday. If you're here by then, you've got a lift to Alaska."

It was Monday night.

*   *   *

After three weeks of non-stop travel, we had been looking forward to a few hours of relaxation; now we were in a race against the clock again. We finally had our lift to Alaska, but we only had thirty-six hours to get 2,500 miles to Seattle.

Then, just as the North Laurel Jaguars posed for a team photo with their newly acquired championship trophy, a guy named Lloyd called to offer us a ride. Lloyd told us that he would drive us a few hours up the road to Frankfort, Kentucky, which would be our twenty-sixth state capitol.

We had pieces of a plan; we just needed to put them together.

Scotty had been frantically working on the other puzzle pieces since Josh's phone call. Near the beginning of the trip, one of our drivers who worked for Southwest Airlines had generously offered us some one-way standby passes if we ever found ourselves in a jam. Scotty was trying to cash those in, but soon learned that the nearest airport we could fly out of was Columbus, Ohio—another three hundred miles away. Furthermore, we couldn't travel to Ohio without first visiting Charleston, West Virginia, or we'd have to spend several days backtracking later in the trip. We briefly considered editing our web site to read "Hitch 49," but decided we should just try to find a way of getting to West Virginia before traveling on to Columbus.

Before our trip, we hadn't known much about Frankfort, the state capitol of Kentucky. We had reason to believe, however, that there wasn't much going on there. Two weeks earlier, the now-defunct Current TV had aired a short piece about our trip. The closing lines to the Current TV spot were:

> *The boys have sweetened the deal with a Golden Ticket. They will randomly choose one of their drivers and fly them and a friend to their final state capital. That's pretty sweet if it's Honolulu, Hawaii; not so much if it's Frankfort, Kentucky.*

That line had been pretty much the only mention of Frankfort on our trip. As Lloyd drove us through the deserted streets, a quick look around town proved the accuracy of our expectations: there wasn't much happening there. More to the point, there wasn't anybody who looked like they wanted to stay up all night driving some foreign hitchhikers to Charleston, West Virginia.

Lloyd was from Hazard, Kentucky. When *The Dukes of Hazzard* became popular, a lot of fans started looking for the fictional Hazzard County in Georgia where the show was set; Hazard, Kentucky was the closest thing in real life. During the ride back to his house, this gave us a great opportunity to ask him really ignorant questions about where he grew up.

"Do you jump cars a lot?"

"Have you ever jumped *this* car?"

"Are you really good at driving at high speed around hairpin corners?"

This served as a release for all the equally uninformed questions we had fielded about our Canadian origins over the past month.

"The only traffic that'll be goin' into West Virginia 'round this time of night is truckers," said Lloyd. "If you guys want, we can try the CB radio in my Jeep. We might be able to flag somebody down."

Of course Lloyd had a CB in a jacked-up, mud-speckled red Jeep parked in his driveway. He was from Hazard, after all. As far as we knew, CB radios—not cellphones—were standard issue in rural Kentucky. How else could you taunt the Sheriff as he chased you rally-style around sharp corners on a dirt road?

We all huddled into Lloyd's Jeep. He adjusted the CB radio to the channel that all the truckers use on the roads, something that is common knowledge in Lloyd's world. He "tweaked the squelch out" so we could reach as far as possible, and instantly we heard some truckers bantering over the airwaves. Lloyd instantly transformed into a seasoned CB radio veteran. His accent thickened and he began to speak with even more southern country flavor than before.

"Hey y'all, who's got their ears on? Anyone goin' east to West Virginy tonight? C'mon back now, y'all."

There was a brief pause and then the truckers continued their conversation about hunting. Around that time of the year, hunting was the topic of choice for most blue-collar Kentucky folk. Judging by the road-killed deer we had seen along the highways in that state, I suspect that driving a rig would almost be considered hunting.

"C'mon now, I know y'all can hear me."

The CB idea, which had seemed like a good one at first, turned into a game of listening to the ridiculous banter and accents over the CB channel. Trying to convince southern truckers to go out of their way to pick up two men in the middle of the night proved to be a task even Lloyd's CB radio skills couldn't handle. The radio didn't get us a ride, but at least it provided some entertainment.

It was time for us to leave for the increasingly vacant highway and stand at the side until we got lucky, or to try and find a motel. Neither of those options sounded enticing, and we were having fun visiting with Lloyd, so we lingered in his driveway chatting with him. It turned out that although the CB radio hadn't panned out for us, Lloyd had yet another ace up his sleeve.

At one point, after a long pause in the conversation, Lloyd appeared to get lost in deep thought. We followed his gaze down the block toward an object that could potentially salvage our hopes of flying to Alaska in two days.

"Well, I suppose since I can't drive you, and I need to take my Jeep to work tomorrow, you might be able to have …" Lloyd paused for a moment, considering if what he was about to suggest was a good idea. "… *that*."

Unless you operate the electromagnet at a scrap yard, a heavily dented '95 Geo Prizm with a filthy interior and a busted headlight isn't the sort of vehicle that brings a smile to your face. But tonight, under those yellow southern streetlights, that junker was simply beautiful.

Neither of us knew what to say. What exactly did he mean by "have"?

"I just bought it for fifty bucks off my sister because she was broke," Lloyd explained. "I honestly don't care what happens to it."

This was probably the best offer of the trip. Sure, Josh had offered us a ride to Alaska in his Cessna just hours earlier, but he was going there anyway and had extra seats. Lloyd was offering us a vehicle to take—unsupervised—to another town, where he would trust us to leave it for him to pick up later. This was true generosity. Maybe that's how they do things in Hazard.

This would still count as hitchhiking, too, because it didn't violate any of the three rules we had made with Kyle before leaving on the trip:

1.   We had to visit all fifty state capitol buildings.

2.   We had to do it in less than fifty days.

3.   We could not pay for any transportation at any point in the trip.

We sealed the deal with a handshake, but we didn't even make it off Lloyd's block before we simultaneously announced to one another that we should take this car a bit further than Lloyd had suggested. When he'd said, "I honestly don't care what happens to it," we had both known that we'd be taking it to West Virginia, solving our problem in one sleep-deprived fell swoop.

Worst-case scenarios raced through our heads. What if the car broke down? Was it okay to leave it at the side of the road and hitch another ride? When we thought about it, having a broken-down vehicle beside us might be a great way to get a ride out of pity. But what would happen if we got pulled over? Who should we say the car belonged to? Whose car was it, really? Would Lloyd be angry?

We pondered those thoughts as we drove through the night, finally arriving in Charleston, West Virginia to obtain our precious photos of us in front of its state capitol building. Then we turned around and drove back toward Kentucky, hoping there would be enough gas to make it to the place Lloyd had told us to leave the car. He would be out the better part of a tank of gas, but we could make that up to him after the trip.

We drove to the town of Morehead and found a parking lot to ditch the car. I tucked the keys under the driver's side tire and we walked to the on-ramp. Scotty found some empty pizza boxes nearby and started making a sign that said OHIO. We were back to more conventional hitchhiking.

The rain picked up. People rode horses peacefully in the field behind us. The hours passed. Things weren't looking good.

"Okay," I said finally. "I didn't want to mention this before, because we've already taken that car so far, but ..."

"But what? We can't take that car anywhere. It's running on fumes right now. Lloyd will be lucky if he gets it to a gas station."

"Yeah, but here's the thing. When I checked the registration to make sure his story about that car was true, I noticed a five-dollar bill in the glove compartment. I also saw a few dollars in quarters in the ashtray, and more loose change on the floor. It's a pretty sleazy move, but since the money was in the car, we wouldn't be paying for any transportation."

We raced back to the car and rifled through every nook and cranny where spare change might conceivably be found. After we had gathered it up, we counted $9.80. It would have to be enough. We fueled up, handed over "our" change to a gas station attendant, and headed north as quickly as the Geo's sketchy steering could handle in the downpour.

We decided to leave it in Covington, a southern suburb on the Kentucky side of the Licking River. It didn't take long to realize this was a low-income neighborhood. We considered buying a bottle of nice whisky to leave Lloyd as a token of our gratitude, but concluded that putting a bottle of whisky in his car would nearly double its value to any would-be car thief.

We pulled into a grocery store parking lot and called our next drivers: a pair of college students from Cincinnati named Tori and Greg, who were already on their way to meet us. They had called the day before to ask if we needed a ride to Columbus, but could only come as far as the Ohio border to pick us up.

Tori and Greg finally arrived. We convinced them to drive fast so that we could stop at the Ohio state capitol building for the requisite photos and still make our flight. That ride was a blur. We nearly broke our rule of never sleeping during a ride; we usually tried to be as upbeat and fun as possible, but at this point we had about as much gas in our tanks as Lloyd's Geo.

*   *   *

The street signs in Columbus indicated that we were at the right corner, but it wasn't immediately apparent where the capitol building was.

"It should be right over there," said Scotty, "but that building looks like a bank."

A sign near the sidewalk confirmed that the "bank" was, in fact, the building we were looking for. We parked and raced up the steps for some pictures, and soon learned that the building looked so plain because the entire dome had been taken off for renovations. It was hard to decide if we were hallucinating in our sleepless haze. How do you lift off the entire top half of a building? We didn't take much time to wonder before we sped off towards the airport.

We pulled up to the domestic departures gate and hurriedly said goodbye to our companions. Once seated on the plane, we gazed out the window to see a witch lifting bags into the cargo hatch. She was wearing all the usual witch garb: pointy black hat, long nose, black cloak, broom. We had been so caught up in making our ridiculous travel plans work that we had completely forgotten it was Halloween. At least we knew that our luggage was on board with us; we watched the witch load our bags onto the plane.

Later that night, we learned that in the split second the witch had exposed Scotty's bag to the sky, the GPS phone inside had managed to send a signal and post it to the map on our web site. For the next several hours, our site showed us on the runway at the Columbus airport. The secret was out: we were getting on a plane. People e-mailed us with guesses as to where we were going. There were some interesting theories—some people even thought we were throwing in the towel and going home.

The next afternoon, as we prepared for a twelve-hour low-level flight to Alaska in Josh's Cessna, we took some time to let the events of the last few weeks sink in. Josh was going to drop us off in Juneau, Alaska; this would be our twenty-ninth state capitol. It's also a town that is only accessible by boat or air—there are no roads to hitchhike out of Juneau. It was November, we were traveling to Alaska, and I didn't even have a jacket. But we had the next twelve hours in a loud, cold airplane with no bathroom breaks to come up with solutions to those problems. And we loved every second of it.

Matt Fidler and his companion Scott MacDonald touched down in Honolulu, Hawaii exactly fifty days after leaving Times Square in New York. A Los Angeles band threw a Hitch 50 wrap-up concert on day forty-nine and bought them tickets to Hawaii with the proceeds. Now, years after graduating with a Bachelor of Commerce Degree, Matt is a bachelor but has not yet conducted any significant commerce.

Patagonian Express

Encountering the world's worst driver on a remote South American highway.

By George Kalli & Ashley Reed Kalli

The Carretera Austral in Chile is a 1,240-kilometer, mostly gravel highway that was built in the 1980s during the dictatorship of President Augusto Pinochet. The highway traverses the western front of the Andes in the country's southernmost reaches until its progress is blocked by two of the largest icefields outside Antarctica.

While staying on the island of Chiloe over Christmas, my girlfriend Ashley and I decided that we wanted to travel the Carretera Austral. Reading about the highway in our guidebook brought to mind some of the more remote and mountainous highways in our home state of Alaska; on these roads you should always carry spare tires, fuel, and water, and be prepared to assist disabled vehicles. We decided to travel by bus.

From Chiloe, we took a ferry to the town of Chaiten to access the northern end of the highway. Upon arriving in Chaiten, we discovered that one of their tourist buses was broken and the other had "disappeared." Undeterred, we spent a few hours trying to hitch a ride until the falling darkness and dropping temperature chased us inside.

We got up the next morning to await the latest bus gossip. While we stood in the icy rain, an Israeli man named Eti approached us with a proposition: did we want to share the cost of a car to the Futaleufú River? The Futaleufú, known as "the river painted by God," is a world-class rafting river, and Eti was hoping to join a rafting trip that afternoon. He meant business. He wanted desperately to go rafting, but he had to make it back to Chaiten the same day in order to continue on a tour departing the next morning. Traveling to Futaleufú hadn't been our original plan, but it sounded better than staying in Chaiten for another day, so we agreed.

Eti had already found the vehicle that would become our Patagonian Express—a Honda Accord. We watched as the owner, a man in a yellow suit, showed our driver how to operate the vehicle. The driver, Jorge, was an overweight man who looked about fifty. He had bushy hair with a streak of gray on top, and an excess of nose and ear hairs. His chauffeur's uniform consisted of a sweatshirt and sweatpants decorated with mayonnaise stains, and brown slippers worn over white cotton gym socks.

We climbed into the car and watched Jorge fumble with the shifter. The owner promptly returned and offered more instructions, leaning in and pointing to various instruments and controls. Jorge was apparently having trouble figuring out how the vehicle worked.

"Doesn't he know how to drive a stick-shift?" I said to Ashley.

"It's not a stick," she whispered. "It's an automatic."

Perhaps that should have been ample warning that we should get out of the vehicle before it was too late. But it wasn't, and we didn't.

It soon became evident that Jorge was an excitable fellow who liked to emphasize key points by gesticulating wildly with his hands. Perhaps he thought these gestures would help us understand his Spanish. As we left Chaiten, he waved his arms excitedly, shouting about the former dictator Pinochet.

The first problem was the windshield, which fogged up completely in the rain. I showed Jorge the defrost button and he began gesticulating wildly, perhaps exclaiming that he thought I was a genius.

As the windshield cleared, Jorge stepped harder on the gas pedal and we began fishtailing precariously from side to side on the curvy gravel highway. We almost went off the road twice, and on a third occasion we sideswiped a guardrail. Even while driving at a hundred kilometers an hour, Jorge also seemed disinclined to perform any steering maneuvers—which meant we ran over several huge rocks. I felt one with my feet as it smashed against the floorboard.

Jorge frequently forgot that he was driving an automatic and shifted, seemingly at random, between Drive, D2, Neutral, and Reverse. Yes, *reverse*. Whenever he hit reverse the transmission would seize up and the car would either lurch into a skid or completely die. After he did this a few times, the transmission began slipping.

Things went from bad to worse. A few minutes later we caught some air off the end of a bridge and the car bottomed out with a violent *thud!* After that the suspension was shot, so we bottomed out a lot more. Our crash landing also seemed to affect the transmission: the next time Jorge shifted into reverse while going eighty kilometers per hour, he couldn't get it started at all. Luckily, this was only because the landing had knocked the cables off the battery terminals. That much I was able to fix.

Jorge's next trick was taking the wrong road and trying to pull a U-turn, which ended when he high-centered the car on the highway median. Half the car was hanging off on either side, so we all had to get out and push it back onto the road. The exhaust pipe got separated from the muffler in the process, and after that you could hear the Accord's unmuffled roar from a long ways off.

Jorge high-centered the car again a few minutes later, but this time he simply hit the gas and we took off with gravel flying. This must have dented the transmission pan, because after that Jorge couldn't shift from park to reverse without strong-arming the shifter, which caused a horrible grinding noise.

All of this was happening with the heat blasting at full strength, which was no problem while Jorge could roll his window up and down to control the temperature. But the window eventually jammed in the upright position, which elicited a "Qué calor!" from Jorge every thirty seconds after that. The rain ended and the sun came out, but rather than turn the heat off, Jorge simply sat there sweating and periodically fumbling with the window knob.

When we eventually got close to our destination, Jorge remembered that he didn't really know where he was going. So he began stopping at driveways and shouting out the window at people, asking them for directions. This took some time, especially since every time he saw somebody he recognized—which was just about everybody—he slammed on the brakes, jumped out, hugged them, and exchanged a few pleasantries.

We eventually found the rafting company Eti was looking for, dropped him off, and then continued with Jorge into town. He explained that a friend of his worked at another rafting company, and that he might be able to get us on a trip.

When we pulled up to the company's office, I recognized it from a magazine article I had read. It catered to movie-star clients like Demi Moore and Sharon Stone, who spend upward of five thousand dollars for a single trip. I knew we weren't the company's target market, but Jorge seemed confident, so we got out of the car and followed him down the driveway toward the office.

Inexplicably, partway down the driveway we found a huge butcher's knife laying in the middle of the gravel, glistening in the sunlight. Before we could stop him, Jorge picked up the knife and started jogging toward the outdoor dining patio and sauna of the multi-thousand-dollar-per-trip movie-star rafting company— wearing mayonnaise-stained sweats, waving a butcher's knife, and yelling "Hola! Hola!"

Needless to say, the staff was not amused. An American employee told Jorge, rather gruffly, that his friend was out on the river, and that he couldn't come barging into the resort bothering clients. Jorge looked dejected and handed over the butcher's knife. We shrugged and told the man that Jorge was our driver and we were trying to reach Futaleufú.

So Jorge drove us into town. We were pretty happy when we arrived.

Hours later, while eating dinner, we heard the roar of jet engines. When we looked out the window, we saw Jorge driving the poor Accord down the block, which we watched with detached horror. By this time the brake lights weren't working. The haunting sounds of the car's mechanical squeals and mournful exhaust note stayed with us long after it disappeared.

With the exception of a demolition derby, Ashley and I have never witnessed such rapid annihilation of a vehicle. We sometimes wonder if Jorge ever made it back to Chaiten. If he did, I expect his friend in the yellow suit did not remain his friend for long.

George and Ashley met in an Alaska fishermans' bar, and later spent a year traveling through South America together. They got engaged during the trip—while hiking in the shadow of a smoldering volcano—and now live happily in Anchorage, Alaska. George is currently putting the finishing touches on a book about their journey.

Air Apparent

Customer service is not their specialty.

By Rhian Knowles

I consider myself to be a seasoned plane traveler, if only because I once took fifteen domestic and international flights in a three-month period. I am confident in saying that I've experienced both ends of the travel spectrum, regardless of whether I wanted to or not. I have experienced metal detectors that don't have issues with my metal hair clips and the zips on my cargo pants, and others that go berserk to the point where I am all but stripped down and airport security are salivating at the thought of making a drug bust.

So consider taking a few pointers from me: if you have a long flight coming up and can't afford to fly first class, start training for it now by finding the smallest seat you can, and then squeezing yourself into it. Do this for several hours each day. Then buy some Nytol and start taking the pills a week before your flight.

One of my more memorable trips began like many others—with a longing to skip the travel portion, and a frantic re-packing of my bag. The flight from Edmonton to Vancouver on Canada's west coast, where I was to meet up with my friend and travel companion, was delayed twice as I sat in the departure lounge in an increasingly agitated state. It got to the point where I was bumped up to first class for the inconvenience, but this was rather eclipsed by the fact that my three-hour layover in Vancouver turned into fifteen minutes. Not much time, you'd probably agree, to dash madly from the domestic terminal to the international departure lounge, carrying a backpack that is repeatedly bruising your leg with every step, while hearing your name announced repeatedly over the loudspeaker by an equally frantic traveling companion.

Jumping off the still-moving airplane from Edmonton, I ran pell-mell through the crowded Vancouver airport, scattering small children and overpriced snack foods. My friend and I had agreed to meet at the downstairs baggage carousel before setting off for the international departure lounge.

As I sped through the concourse, I momentarily debated abandoning my pack and spending three months overseas with nothing but what I was wearing. It was around that time that I became aware of someone next to me, huffing and puffing in synchronized unison. A cursory glance to one side revealed my friend—having given up on our baggage area rendezvous, she had set out for the gate at a sprint. We had both been so focused on making the flight that we hadn't realized we were jogging next to each other for several minutes.

The long-haul flight from Vancouver to Thailand was to be with an airline whose name I cannot mention as the airline, sadly, is still in operation. I shall rename it here as Air Apparent—since apparently they believe they are a first-class airline. I had heard nothing but good about this airline for the past five months, and was actually looking forward to the flight after so many glowing reports.

Looking back, I now feel I may need AA—that would be Airlines Anonymous—to help me recover from my aviation ordeal.

After rushing to reach the gate on time, I collapsed in a sweaty heap on the floor next to an unmoving line. Had I known we were boarding next Tuesday I could have avoided the heart-palpitating thrill of running the length of the airport in three minutes flat. Collapsed on the dusty floor, gasping for air, I tried to imagine myself in my plush airline seat—I knew I would cool down on the plane, since I always find them cold.

Little did I know.

If I were to make up my own version of the flight attendant's announcements, they would start something like this:

> *Ladies and gentlemen, good afternoon and welcome to Air Apparent, the second-best airline in the world as voted by you, our passengers. As you board, you will notice that we have moderated the temperature to a balmy thirty-five degrees Celsius in order to simulate Thailand's climate in a closed environment. To ensure your continued acclimatization, we will be turning the heat up to a tropical forty-five degrees once we reach our cruising altitude.*

Never in my life have I been on a plane that was so hot. Coupled with lighting that was for some reason a bit dim, it gave the overall effect of a gigantic tubular sauna. Collapsing into my child-sized seat, I reached upwards for the tiny, personal air-conditioning vent all airplanes have. Usually my first move is to turn these off, but today I was going to crank that baby wide open.

As my fingers scrabbled in vain against the hard plastic, I discovered that there *were* no air vents. The plane was *that* old. There was only a single vent running the length of the plane, giving off a feeble hissing noise—probably to create the illusion of air movement. Placing my hand near this vent confirmed my suspicions: it was obvious that if air conditioning had ever existed on this airplane, it had stopped working some time ago—probably about the same time the plane was built, which I imagined was several decades ago.

Giving up in despair, I tried to focus my attention on the safety demonstration mandatory on all flights.

For your convenience, we would like to direct your attention to the television screens at the front of each section. For those of you seated in rows other than row one, this would be the thin strip of white light you can see above the other passengers' heads. We hope you brought a good book. Of course, most of the wires in this airplane are crossed. So if you are sitting in row 12, seat B, you will need to find row 651, seat Q, in order to turn on your light. Please be considerate of your fellow passengers during this exercise in futility.

I reached up to turn on my reading light, but as the wires for our lights were apparently crossed, my friend's flickered on instead. Rather than climbing into her lap to read, I tried to think of something else to do. As I struggled to remove as much clothing as possible without being indecent, a smiling flight attendant came by, checked my seat number, and inquired about a drink preference for my special vegetarian meal. At least the request I had made when booking the flight had been received, so that was one thing that was going right.

How silly of me to be so optimistic. After an incomprehensible welcome speech from the pilot, who could have been quoting his favorite golf statistics for all I know, the plane eased back from the gate and taxied down the runway.

As we begin endlessly taxiing momentarily, in preparation for taking off tomorrow, we ask that you return all trays to their upright positions. Unless your tray is broken, in which case we ask that you rest it uncomfortably on your knees for the entire flight.

After a long wait, the pilot finally taxied and coaxed the plane into the air. With my tray table resting uncomfortably on my knees, I remembered my Nytol and tried to find it, digging feverishly through my pack with one finger (about all I could move).

A slightly less smiley flight attendant walked by with my special meal, well ahead of the meals for the other passengers. Smiling encouragingly, I tried to catch her eye to confirm that yes, I was the passenger she was looking for and had spoken to earlier. Apparently, either seat K47 had moved or I had become invisible. After three trips up and down the aisle, during which I performed all manner of twitches in my seat to catch her attention (the seat being too small to do anything else), I finally received my meal ... but wished I hadn't.

Both my friend and I ended up getting sick, quite possibly from the combination of the food and the overheated plane. We had different meals—mine vegetarian, hers with meat—so I guess it was a cross-meal contamination. I suppose I should have been suspicious when I received an unidentifiable main course (which resembled a few limp carrots peeking through what looked like congealed ketchup), three grapes, mushy melon, frozen bread, melted butter, and plastic cutlery that snapped halfway through the meal. After I downed what I could, I then had to sit with the remnants of my feast on my lap and wait while the rest of the passengers were served their meals and ate them before the trays were cleared away.

One meal and several hours into the flight, an insidious aroma started creeping through the cabin. The toilet, which we were seated near, had started to disperse its odor. Of course, it could have been the elderly women seated next to me, but I wasn't about to initiate that conversation. Periodically, this same woman rubbed some sort of strange-smelling liquid onto her legs; combined with the other unknown smell, this was enough to make my eyes water and my lungs reflexively convulse. Interpreting (correctly) my befuddled glance, our seatmate confided that the paint thinner was to help improve the circulation in her legs (apparently to the detriment of air circulating in the lungs of nearby passengers). Nevertheless, we made the best of the situation by inventing a new game called Where's That Smell Coming From?

As the flight wore on, my nerves became raw. Other passengers shared my misery: many had a noticeable sheen of sweat on their faces. Babies cried. The toilet stank. Paint Thinner Lady began a twice-hourly application of her circulation-improving miracle liquid. As my body swelled from the heat and my stomach convulsed, my seat began to shrink—I swear it did. I tried listening to my friend's mp3 player, but it only held fifty-six songs. I tried banging my head against the side of the plane to knock myself out, but only succeeded in giving myself a headache.

As I buried my face in the miniature airline pillow and wept with deep and sobbing cries, another incomprehensible announcement by the captain preceded the lights going out. Either it was nighttime, or someone had tried turning on their reading light, which overloaded the only two circuits installed on the plane.

I eventually unearthed my Nytol, which was buried at the very bottom of my overstuffed pack, took two, and remained rigidly awake for the remainder of the flight.

Ladies and gentleman, we are now beginning our descent into Hong Kong. Once again, thank you for flying with Air Apparent, voted the second-best airline in the world by you, our passengers. Please do remember us to your family and friends.

I have—but probably not in the way the airline intended.

Rhian Knowles was bitten at a young age by a particularly virulent travel bug, for which there is no known cure. To alleviate the worst of the symptoms she travels regularly. Most notably, Rhian has survived a hurricane in Cuba and unsuccessfully rafted a seven-meter waterfall in New Zealand.

The Old (Sort Of) Wild West

A place where fact and fiction happily converge.

By Philip Torrens

As a writer,* I know well the temptation—as the Irish so delicately put it—to not let the truth get in the way of a good story. My own license to get creative, however, has always consisted of minor embellishments to real personal experiences. A dash of hyperbole here. A judicious rearranging of chronology there. Purely for the sake of narrative flow, of course.

Yet my amateur efforts pale in comparison to those of a German named Karl May (pronounced "my") and his so-called "experiences."

Karl was the master of a skill best referred to as Completely Making It Up. Born in Germany in 1842, Karl experienced a Dickensian childhood. He endured poverty, a sadistic father, the death of several younger siblings, and years of blindness caused by a vitamin-deficient diet. He found solace in listening to fairy tales his grandmother would spin for him. Later, with his sight restored, he escaped life's bitter routine by reading books from the local library. His tastes leaned toward the pulp fiction of his day: *Rinaldo Rinaldini, the Chief of Robbers; Himlo Himlini, the Chief of Robbers in Spain; Sallo Salini, the Most Formidable Chief of Robbers*; and on and on and on.

By the time Karl was sixteen, the foundations for his rich fantasy life had been solidly laid. He had become fascinated by the "wild savages" of North America, and it was around this time that he wrote and submitted his first story about "Indians" to a magazine. (It was rejected and has since been lost.)

By 1861 Karl had scrabbled his way to a teaching certificate, which was revoked soon after he was convicted of theft. He spent six weeks in prison. He claimed to be the victim of an unfortunate misunderstanding over the ownership of a roommate's pocket watch, even though similar "misunderstandings" would dodge Karl for many years.

Feeling that society had wronged him, Karl embarked on the life of a not-so-master criminal—in his case, as a con artist. Deeming it unjust that the practice of medicine should be restricted to those who'd actually gone to medical school, he practiced briefly as a doctor. (In spite of—or perhaps because of—his earlier blindness, Karl opted to specialize: he impersonated an ophthalmologist.)

Shortly afterwards, he skinned several local furriers by having coats delivered "on approval" to his hotel room, then making off with them. He was busted while pawning his ill-gotten gains and packed off to the pokey for another four years. He made good use of this time, developing his musical talent with the prison church chorus and immersing himself in the prison library. He apparently read many travel narratives and novels about the Wild West, which inspired him to submit more cowboy-and-Indian stories of his own for publication, again without success.

Perhaps inspired by all the police he had rubbed shoulders with over the years, Karl decided that his next career should be as a cop. As a phony flatfoot, he began seizing banknotes from innocent citizens, claiming the bills were forgeries. Got that? A counterfeit cop confiscating *real* money as counterfeit cash. This hall-of-mirrors scenario was typical of Karl's adult life: the boundaries between real life and make-believe became increasingly blurred.

In 1892 he got a big break: his first Western book was published. From then on he never looked back, cranking out seventy books over the balance of his life, many of them Westerns. Any lesser man might have been daunted by the fact that he'd never actually, you know, been to North America. Or, so far as we know, even set eyes on a Native American. But not our hero. He brought that same "can-do" attitude to these projects that he had applied to all the other professions he'd "practiced." Indeed, he wrote so assuredly and convincingly of life on the plains that many readers were certain his was the voice of first-hand experience.

Karl's most popular western characters included Old Shatterhand, an American pioneer descended from Germans, and Winnetou, a noble Indian chief, or *roten* (red) gentleman. In later years, Old Shatterhand became a kind of alter ego for Karl, who convinced his adoring fans that Shatterhand's adventures were his own. It seems more than likely that somewhere along the line he also convinced himself, and was no longer consciously pulling a con. The fact that Shatterhand's adventures are first-person narratives probably speeded this process: Karl would have spent many long days "in character" as he was writing.

Where the heroes of antiquity had their magic swords, Old Shatterhand had two latter-day Excaliburs: the fictional rifles Bärentöter (Bear Killer) and Henrystutzen (Henry Carbine). The Henrystutzen could supposedly fire twenty-five shots without reloading—far more than any real gun of the day. Karl's contemporary, Sigmund Freud, would have had a field day with the implications of that.

May's mythic Indians were enormously appealing to German readers, who saw in them kindred spirits to their own imagined Teutonic ancestors—rugged individualists uncorrupted by civilization. Aryan and Indian were equal, as far as they were concerned. And in fact, Old Shatterhand and Winnetou become blood brothers during the course of the books.

Karl's first authenticated visit to North America wasn't until 1908, long after his supposed adventures there had made him famous and wealthy. There's no evidence he ever got any further west than (appropriately) Buffalo, New York. Even a century ago, that was hardly the wild frontier. Or at least not of the sort Karl had made famous.

Given his rough start, it's nice to report that Karl had some happiness later in life. After his first marriage ended in divorce, he enjoyed the companionship of a woman who would today be called a trophy wife: Klara, a widow twenty years his junior. His books made him rich enough to purchase a house, which he dubbed Villa Shatterhand. Karl died there in 1912, but his influence lives on.

Thanks in large part to Karl's writing, to this day Germany is home to vast tribes of *Indianers*—groups of otherwise respectable people who periodically meet to swap their lederhosen for loincloths, live in tepees, and generally go native.

Several years back, I met a couple of authentic Canadian Indians (or First Nations people, as they are known here) who had scored some serious wampum traveling to Germany as special guest stars for these powwows. These Natives were real characters. Their eyes gleamed with mischief, and it was obvious they loved nothing better than to see how tall a tale they could make you swallow. But they understood what their German hosts expected: stoic, laconic, noble savages. So that's what they gave them. Call it native intelligence on the part of these wily redskins; they knew what side their schnitzel was breaded on.

Lest we North Americans get too smug about these fairytales of the Old West, I should mention a place in the Rocky Mountains that offers the opportunity to sleep in "authentic" teepees ... made of cement. As far as I know, teepees were used only by Plains and Foothills tribes. And they certainly weren't made of concrete.

Karl's legacy also lives on through the silver screen. From 1912 into the late 1960s, European studios churned out nearly two dozen films based on his novels. They seem to occupy the same place in the European "Western" pantheon as John Wayne films do in North America—except that in May's Wild West, the Natives are heroes, not brutish enemies or comic sidekicks. Hollywood wouldn't get so progressive until the 1990 film *Dances With Wolves*.

Fittingly, not one of the films based on May's books was actually shot in North America: various locations in Yugoslavia and Spain impersonated the Wild West. Old Karl would have understood—and approved.

Philip Torrens is fond of the frontier himself. Some believe he was raised by wolves and then adopted by the very, very last of the Mohicans. His Indian name can be freely translated as "That-tracking-clue-which-a-missing-horse-leaves-behind."

Tanzanian Tantrums

An African safari can make a grown man cry.

By Philip Blazdell

Things started going wrong before I even left the UK. The Kenyan embassy had "lost" my passport, the bank had canceled my credit card, and my traveler's checks still hadn't arrived. As I pushed myself through the throngs of happy Christmas shoppers along London's Oxford Street, I grew increasingly concerned that I might have to spend Christmas in the UK after all.

Wearily, I dragged myself to the section of the embassy that deals with travel visas, where I was greeted by a smiling guard.

"*Jambo,*" I said. "How are you?"

"*Jambo jambo,*" he said, smiling back as he handed me my passport.

I had been to the embassy so many times in the last few days that our exchange felt like saying goodbye to an old friend. I shook his hand and pushed back into London crowds.

Within a few hours I had packed my things and squeezed myself into a crowded tube train. The commuter next to me, a man in a pinstriped suit, eyed my bulging rucksack, my combat boots, and my T-shirt.

"You do know it's snowing," he said, as I cleaned my sunglasses. And then, before I could answer, "Going home for Christmas?"

"No, East Africa," I replied. This obviously upset him, because he promptly returned to his crossword puzzle.

A few days later I was sipping cool Tusker beer on a veranda in Kenya. It had been some time since my last trip to Africa, and I was glad to see that things hadn't changed too much. The people were still rioting, the economy had more holes in it than Dutch cheese, and Tusker beer was still the best beer in the entire universe.

Things were going to plan. I was away from the UK, no one had mentioned Christmas to me, and I had no mobile phone or pager to constantly stress me out. More importantly, the barman was attentive to my needs: "Will that be one crate or two this evening, sir?"

Good conversation, the warm night air, and delicious food lulled me into a sense of false security. I began to relax, which is probably why when a group of fellow travelers I'd met at the hotel suggested hiring a Land Rover and spending a few days in the Ngorongoro Conservation Area, I readily agreed to join them. A quick dip into the guidebook revealed that the crater has been compared to Noah's Ark and the Garden of Eden—and has the added advantage of actually existing.

Today, Noah might be a bit disappointed by dwindling animal numbers, but he'd have no trouble finding lions, elephants, rhinos, buffalo, and many of the plains herbivores such as wildebeest, Thomson's gazelle, zebra, and reedbuck. Thousands of flamingos wade in the shallows of Lake Magadi, the soda lake on the floor of the crater.

The guidebook said nothing about stranded Land Rovers, something we would certainly see a lot of over the next few days.

Our group picked up five Land Rovers—with drivers—just outside the small town of Arusha. The light rain that had followed me since London turned into heavy squalls. As we scurried around town buying food and beers for the two-day expedition, locals crouched under makeshift tarpaulin shelters and complained about the "worst rains to hit East Africa in years." As a last-minute thought, I grabbed a Swahili phrasebook from a beautiful *Kanga*-clad local.

A few hours later we were bouncing through scrub brush on our way to the crater. Our driver spent most of his time with one hand on the wheel and one hand trying to eject an Elton John tape from the cassette deck. He seemed to hit every pothole and rock in the road, which was not surprising, really, as he spent more time facing backwards to chat with us than he did looking at what obstacles lay ahead. Encouraged by our shouts, he floored the aging Landy and sent us spinning along streambeds, flying over rocks and into every mud pool he could find.

Wedged into the back seat in and among all our gear, I was quite safe, so as a precautionary measure our "mobile bar," which had been bouncing away on the front "suicide" seat, was passed back to me.

We arrived at our campsite—the beautifully named Safari Junction—just as the sun was setting, and I quickly laid the bar out on the rust-red road and made cocktails for everyone. Apart from a few bruised bottoms and a rather unfortunate incident with a bottle of tequila, we were in good spirits. Only a good night's sleep separated us from the crater and some magnificent game viewing. Contentedly, I finished my sixth sundowner and retired to my tent. The big African sky was now studded with stars, and I spent a happy hour trying in vain to find the Southern Cross.

Later, a storm woke me. The heavens were streaked with wild, forked bolts of lightning. Ominous claps of thunder rolled round the hills, and rain came down in Biblical proportions. In my intoxicated state, all I could do was smile and think about the poor commuters in London.

The next day the sky was clear, and in the early morning mist the world looked new and ready for conquest. My peaceful thoughts, which already lacked some coherence due to the sizable hangover I was nurturing, were shattered by our overzealous driver telling me to shake a leg. "*Pole, pole,*" I said to him. ("Slowly, slowly.") This caused much laughter and backslapping among the other drivers.

The journey to the entrance of the crater was uneventful, a long, hot drive through rough scrubland, only livened when our eagle-eyed driver suddenly slammed on the brakes. This would not have been a problem if we hadn't been on a hairpin turn at the time, and if I had not been trying to fix the first cocktails of the day. Malibu and gin flew everywhere.

The driver turned down his Elton John tape for a few seconds and scanned the horizon with his binoculars. A tense silence descended on our small group as we waited to see our first animal (and to see how much gin I could salvage).

After what seemed like hours, our driver dropped his binoculars and let rip with a real belly laugh. Between convulsions, he explained that he had mistaken a tree for an elephant, and the funny thing was he had made the same mistake the previous week.

In retrospect, this should have set off all kinds of alarm bells.

The descent into the actual crater was somewhat of an anticlimax. Through the haze of the mid-morning heat, I could just make out thousands of flamingos wading in the shallows of Lake Magadi, a sight I had fallen in love with the first time I had seen it from a 747 when I landed in Mombassa many years before. The sight, which had lived in my dreams for so long, gradually came into focus below me.

It was then that I realized it was Christmas Eve.

The bottom of the crater is a different world, both from an ecological and a philosophical standpoint. The crater is no longer teeming with game as it once was, but it is still a place where you can see game in a relatively undisturbed environment. Few memories remain as vivid for me as sitting on top of our Land Rover beside the shores of Lake Magadi that day, contentedly watching the hippos play. I had seen hippos in Africa before, but never so close and never in such a relaxed state. I must have been lost in thought, because I failed to notice that a rare black rhino had approached, obviously as keen to examine us as we were to watch him.

The weather, which up to that point had been hot and sunny, was becoming less appealing. Many feet above us, around the top of the crater, we could see thick storm clouds swirling. We asked the driver if this was going to be a problem, but he just smiled his most enigmatic smile, shrugged his shoulders, and drove the Land Rover further into the middle of the crater in search of more game.

"Closer, closer!" we urged him as he inched toward a herd of zebras, who were having none of it and bolted away.

The driver, never one to give up, gave rapid pursuit, leaving us clinging for dear life to the top of the Land Rover. In an attempt to get in front of the herd, he aimed the Landy at a small gully with a dry riverbed. What he had not remembered was that last night's torrential rain had flooded this gully. We suddenly found ourselves axle-deep in mud.

All of us piled out and began to dig under the back wheels. The zebras looked on with puzzled expressions. After some time grunting and tossing spadefuls of sticky red mud, one of my traveling companions named Mike took a break to fiddle with his camera and asked the driver, "These zebras aren't dangerous, are they?"

The driver, who had by now ejected the Elton John tape, replied, "No, but the lion we saw one hundred meters back is."

We dug much faster after that.

All this digging didn't help much, and by the time the other Land Rovers in our convoy arrived, we were plastered from head to toe in mud.

The first Land Rover of the convoy attempted to push us out—which, even to me, seemed not very sensible—and soon we had two Land Rovers stuck in the muddy riverbed, sinking slowly.

"Save the alcohol!" my friends yelled at me.

Eventually a rope was found, and as the rain once again began in earnest, we fastened one end to our rapidly sinking vehicle and the other to one of the other Land Rovers. I was too slow getting out of the way, and the spinning wheels covered me with a fresh coating of mud. Nevertheless, our Land Rover slowly but surely eased its way out.

The second Land Rover, however, was stuck fast. As we tried desperately to get some traction on the rear axle by getting everyone to stand on the bumper, a Land Rover full of Germans from another convoy pulled up to watch. We could have done with their considerable Teutonic bulk, but it was not to be. They looked at us plastered in mud, took a few pictures, laughed, and drove off.

After another thirty minutes of pushing and shoving, the discussion was made to abandon the vehicle. One Land Rover down—four to go.

As the rain came down ever harder, we decided to abandon the safari and follow the German Land Rover back to Arusha. We couldn't see beyond a few feet in front of the windscreen anyway, and driving was becoming more hazardous. Our driver now had two hands firmly on the wheel, and with me hanging out the passenger-side window hollering directions to him, we were making reasonable time toward the only road out of the crater.

Thanks to a combination of skillful driving and my guidance, we managed to miss most of the gullies and streams. However, the ones we didn't miss soaked me in cold mud. After half an hour, I didn't have a clean bit of skin left anywhere; my clothes were drenched, and the thought of my family sitting around the Christmas tree sipping brandies suddenly seemed very attractive.

My misery turned to joy as the German Land Rover, which was grinding away in front of us, suddenly hit a gully and skidded nose-first into a stream. I have never before seen a Land Rover with its rear axle raised at a forty-five degree angle from the ground. It was really quite an impressive sight. We pulled to a stop close by and spent the next few minutes taking pictures of the flustered Germans.

Unfortunately, our driver wanted to help the Germans, so once again I found myself dragged out into the rain to offer an engineer's viewpoint (the next time I go away, I'm going to say I work in a bank). By this time I was cold, miserable, muddy, and completely pissed off. It was instantly obvious that there was no way the Land Rover could be dug out, but still we tried.

One of the Germans was diabetic, so we agreed to take him to Arusha with us; I waded into the three-foot-deep mud hole that surrounded the Land Rover to help him with his belongings. It took some time to convince him that the water wasn't full of killer piranhas, and eventually, reluctantly, he stepped into the water. Shortly after we got back to our Land Rover and were sorting out some cocktails, the German thanked us for the help, but said forlornly that his shoes, which were soaking wet, were ruined.

The temptation to roll him in the mud was nearly too much.

The road out was still passable and we spent the next three hours bouncing along quite happily. The weather cleared, the after-lunch cocktails did the rounds, and I let myself fall into a deep sleep ... until the Land Rover slammed to another sudden halt.

By the time I was fully awake, the driver and my traveling companion were both standing on the hood of the Landy with worried looks on their faces. The main road, which runs almost vertically up a steep slope to the top rim of the crater, had vanished in the rains and was blocked by dozens of trucks and transport vehicles. Nobody was going anywhere.

We joined the queue of traffic and settled in for a long wait. Blankets were laid on top of the now-dry Land Rover and the bar was opened. Our driver wandered among the other drivers trying to find out how long we might have to wait. Various estimates came back: from days to weeks. We smiled each time our driver came back with bad news, shrugged our shoulders as he told his "shit happens, this is Africa, baby" story, and carried on with our quest for the perfect cocktail.

As the sun went down, my impromptu English school and choir broke up and I decided that all things being equal, I could really handle a beer. On top of the hill I could just make out the lights of what I presumed to be a small town. "They must have a pub or something," I said, trying to convince my longsuffering companion Mike to join me. Against his better judgement (and I am never allowed to forget this), we began the long, slow trudge through mud and stalled vehicles in search of beer.

As we climbed, we were treated to a firsthand perspective on the problem. Trucks were trying to climb the hill one at a time. The whole village would get behind a truck and, with one concerted effort, the driver would floor the throttle and the villagers would try to push it up the muddy hill. Sometimes their efforts paid off, and this produced loud cheers from the crowd; sometimes they were not successful, and the vehicle skidded back down the slope, sending villagers diving for dear life.

Eventually we reached the town and found what looked like a suitable place for a beer. We entered cautiously. The smell of dried sweat and yams was thick in the air. It was dark, and while I searched in my pockets for my flashlight, I could sense all around that people were watching us. If there had been men playing darts, I'm sure a dart would have stopped in mid flight.

We made our way to the metal grill-covered bar, where a stern-looking woman stood scowling at us. "Hi, we're from the UK," said Mike, using the careful tone of a man who is seriously wondering if this is a bad move. "Any chance of a Tusker?"

That broke the ice and within a few seconds we were busy shaking hands, slapping backs, and sipping ice-cold beers. The fact that we were actually stuck in the middle of nowhere suddenly seemed unimportant. The chief of the village was summoned, and another round of drinks was ordered. Things were going well.

Word reached the bar that a tractor had been found that could pull our Land Rover up the hill, so I left my friend clutching his beer and went to investigate. Lightning flashed across the sky like a strobe light on a dance floor, and the rain began to fall in earnest again. I walked—or more accurately, slid—down the hill.

Our driver was busily repacking our gear for an assault on the hill. I dived into the passenger seat to give him some much-needed moral support. The tractor had not appeared, but three dozen mud-caked locals were ready to push, so our driver, who was now bored, decided to try anyway. We agreed on a route up, and he fired the engine.

We climbed slowly, spraying mud everywhere. The wheels were slipping and the locals were getting tired, but at least we were moving. Suddenly the wheels found traction and we shot forward up the slope. The driver had not been expecting this, and in an attempt to prevent us from smashing into a tree, he overcorrected to the left, hit a rut, and sent the Landy into a barrel roll.

It all happened in a flash. The floor became the ceiling, the bar went everywhere, and for some reason the stereo suddenly began playing *Nikita* by Elton John. The fact that I could die if the Landy rolled over the edge of the mountain did cross my mind.

I counted one roll, then two rolls before we stopped. Things were still not as they should be, but before I really knew what was happening, hands had reached through the open window and pulled me out. I was placed safety on the side of the track, and with a collective Herculean effort, the villagers righted the precariously balanced Landy. Before I knew what was happening, our driver floored it again and sent it shooting the final distance up the hill.

The rest of the vehicles in our depleted convoy followed shortly, and arrived at the top of the hill just in time to meet Mike, who was by this time screaming and running toward us.

"Drive! Drive!" he yelled as he flung himself through the back window.

Behind the Landy I could see a mob of screaming locals in hot pursuit. Fortunately, he was an experienced runner, though he later confessed that running for his life was a new experience, one he hoped I could share with him someday. According to Mike, he had become entangled in a tense political conversation with some locals, and apparently his innocent, though naïve views were not appreciated.

We slumped into our seats and relaxed. The road back was clear now. The rain was still falling, but with luck we would be back in a few hours. We bounced along through the rainy African night listening to Elton John.

Our driver, who had now been behind the wheel for about nineteen hours, decided to take a shortcut that he said would get us back to camp in an hour. Weary, we agreed, so he swung off the main track and plunged deep into the bush. Once more, I nodded off.

So confident was our driver in his "shortcut" that he failed to notice the river ahead of us. With a sickening *Ker-Sploosh!* he plunged the Landy straight into it.

The initial impact was followed by the sound of our rear axle scraping across the rocky riverbed, which is actually what woke me up from my slumber. By the time water began seeping into the Landy, I was wide awake and helping the others move our belongings onto the roof. There was no hope of ever getting the Landy out, so we sat hunched on the roof, cold, wet, tired, and despondent. We knew we were in for a long wait; a tractor would have to be found in the morning.

Once again I pictured my family gathered around the Christmas tree, singing carols. Even a half-hearted rendition of *Silent Night* did nothing to improve my foul mood.

I was on the verge of crying when out of the torrential rain appeared the most miraculous vision: a brand-new Land Cruiser. It stopped, the electric window slowly descended, and a friendly face appeared. "Going to Arusha?" the driver asked.

Hardly able to believe our luck, we nodded in unison.

"Jump in."

Once we were snug inside the air-conditioned truck and gorging ourselves on the driver's chocolate stash, I began to feel slightly happier.

"You see, the problem is this," said our new friend. "The locals just don't know how to drive out here."

We heartily agreed.

"Unlike my country, Holland, where we all drive so well that..."

We never did hear what he had to say, for at that very moment we hit a rock, which sent his Land Cruiser spinning into a ditch and his trailer into a tree.

Three hours later, after we had collected all his worldly belongings from the surrounding countryside—covering ourselves in a fresh layer of mud in the process—we hit the road again. Just as the sun was rising over a perfectly blue sky, we rolled into Arusha.

Weeks later, I arrived back in London and stopped in at my local pub for a beer.

"Hey, we missed you at Christmas," the barman said. "Had the family over. It was quite terrible, you know..."

Contrary to popular opinion, Philip Blazdell wasn't raised by wolves or savages. He grew up in London, England and was educated by reading and eavesdropping on the conversations of his elders. This perhaps explains his strange view of the world and often-inappropriate choice of footwear. Philip currently divides his time between Middle England (pretty much like Middle Earth minus the Orcs and Hobbits) and obscure little towns in Japan. He is currently obsessed with European countries beginning with 'A' (Albania, Armenia, and Andorra) and still drinks far too much, far too often. His web site is www.philipblazdell.com.

Ride of Passage

Budget travel in the developing world is not for the faint of heart.

By Tricia Duncan

Riding the "local bus" is what some travelers politely refer to as a cross-cultural experience; others may simply refer to it using lots of expletives. Whether you find yourself flying around hairpin turns in the Himalayas, squashed between fellow travelers in the African Savannah who've been showering as infrequently as yourself, or bouncing along a potholed South American jungle road with a spring up your sphincter, there is one thing you can say with absolute certainty: for any traveler worth his or her salt, riding the local bus is an important "rite of passage."

Welcome to an adventurous concoction of death-defying roads, tortuously uncomfortable seats, breathtaking scenery, and a potpourri of colorful characters that you'll meet no other way. Throw in a dash of dysentery, a dose of abnormal cranial pressure, and a commute that may take minutes, a few hours, or even days, and you have a full-blown pilgrimage into the languages and customs of people around the world. What better way could there be to experience firsthand the everyday workings of foreign lives?

I must be honest: I am a tightwad traveler who will always take the most economical means of getting from point A to point B. Invariably I opt for the cheapest local bus going in a given direction with little regard to its condition, the seat-to-passenger ratio, or the fact that it may circumnavigate the entire Himalayan mountain range on roads no wider than the average American sidewalk. This often results in a heart-fluttering journey of several hours (or days) in what amounts to a sardine can on wheels. Notwithstanding the many discomforts, I have learned that as a reward for me miserly ways, the chaos of getting there can be a more memorable experience than the destination.

If you possess good stamina and healthy bowels, have all the time in the world, and love a good adventure, budget transport in a developing country might be just for you.

First off, dismiss any lofty expectations of arriving at your destination on or even near the "suggested" time of arrival. In some countries the bus may not only be minutes late, but a day or more off schedule.

There is also the hazard of getting on the wrong bus. Never mind that you've been waiting for three days without seeing a single gasoline-powered vehicle; if one bus pulls up, at least fourteen more will arrive within the next two minutes. You'll then be faced with a barrage of young men hanging precariously from the side doors, yelling out destinations, trying to coax you on. A given bus may not have even stopped before some of these guys will leap off, grab your bags, and start hoisting them aboard.

When you ask where they are going, they always nod and emphatically say, "Yes, yes!" They always seem to be going to exactly where you want to go. If you are in, say, India, and tell them you want to get dropped in Brazil, they will still say, "Yes, yes!" and nod their heads.

Once aboard, you may feel some pressure to make sure you are on the right bus. Perhaps you wedge yourself into the doorway and try desperately to get the driver's attention using charades, pointing at your map, or attempting to enunciate correctly from the guidebook. He'll undoubtedly nod and say, "Yes, yes," and the next moment you'll be popped from the doorway like a wine cork, the impatient mob rushing in behind you.

As the bus fills, the driver and his posse carefully take into account the number of seats and then multiply this number by five to achieve the total number of paying customers they can squeeze on board. If you are lucky enough to get an aisle seat, you are almost guaranteed to find someone who was not so lucky sitting on your shoulder. And if by some unlikely chance you actually manage to get comfortable, be sure that the seat in front of you will recline, causing you to contemplate putting on your headlamp to perform oral surgery on the person now reclining in your lap.

Once you are settled, you can start enjoying the bustle of life around you. At a busy intersection there may come a loud banging noise directly below your window. Vendors in colorful clothes are yelling the price of empanadas, chai tea, or a "delicious" meal wrapped in a banana leaf. One lucky fellow jumps aboard the bus, sprinting up and down the aisle with a dripping cardboard box of homemade popsicles. All these vendors work hard to make a sale worth a few pennies, but whether they succeed or not, they must often give freely of their goods to the driver and his cohorts.

Besides the vendors, there are always people with *Chicken Soup for the Soul* stories who jump on and off the bus in hopes of finding sympathizers to their cause. A young boy in rags scrambles aboard and explains that he has lost most of his family and desperately needs your help. He sweetly sings a couple of songs, off key, and then passes his hat around. (I'm a sucker for this one, especially if he has the guts to sing to a crowd.)

At the next stop, the boy jumps off and a lady with a tattered black travel bag comes aboard; she has the ultimate cure for any ailment under the sun. For a very cheap price she will sell you this herbal cure-all miracle pill and throw in a special booklet on healthy living and keeping your colon clean. She manages to speak clearly and with conviction about her product for twenty minutes straight, without any pauses, except for dramatic effect. It's an impressive monologue. If she lived in North America, she would probably be making a six-figure salary working for a pharmaceutical company.

As the bus rolls on, passengers come and go. While you may feel uncomfortably out of your element, there's also the unmistakable feeling that your senses are coming alive. There are opportunities galore to practice new languages, sample new foods, smell some unique smells, or just observe the crazy hubbub around you.

I have traveled many thousands of kilometers on "local buses" of the developing world, and have had many adventures. I've experienced border crossings with anxious armed guards; road accidents; religious pilgrimages; sleeping on the floor in the aisle; riding on the roof; animals chewing on my backpack; roosters crowing under my seat. But of all these experiences, one simple journey through the mountains of Peru stands out.

After searching just about every street in the small town and asking for directions several times, I eventually found the old blue shack of a bus station on a hidden back street. I was several hours early and therefore one of the first passengers to buy a ticket, acquiring seat number four. Slowly, the littered parking lot began to fill: people shouted, roosters crowed, pigs grunted, and vendors sold their products. A brightly painted hunk of metal eventually rattled into the station and came to a coughing halt amidst a cloud of dark smoke. The throng of people pushed forward, swaying back and forth before the closed doors. Determined, I jockeyed to hold my position.

A burly man with a faded sports jersey, rolled-up dress pants and flip-flops yelled to the crowd from the bus steps. He proceeded to the side of the bus, where he started jamming oversized bundles and bags into the rusted storage compartment. In went woven baskets filled with produce, then colorful blankets knotted together and overflowing with household goods. As I feared, there was no room left for my large blue backpack. I attempted to smuggle it on board, but the station manager stopped me. He declared it too big and threw it carelessly to a young boy on the roof, along with bags of grain and a hog-tied goat. They struggled to pass up a large, corroded propane tank, and I tried to forget the bus accident statistics I had read in the guidebook.

I joined the stampede onto the bus, rotating my daypack to my front to protect it from any stealthy hands and avoid knocking any poor passenger unconscious. The dirty windshield was a maze of cracks and was outlined with colorful tassels, plastic flowers, and a golden cross. On the red-carpeted dashboard, the Virgin Mary bobbed back and forth to lively Latin music. The driver was leaning out of the window chatting with several cronies. He whacked the side of the bus several times, squeezed back in, and dropped into the seat. He seemed a jovial character; his patterned shirt was open almost to the navel, and his gold chains jingled to the music as he began to sing along.

Moving down the aisle, I stared at the number three and four seats, which were directly behind a wooden partition that divided them from the driver. Although I'm fairly short, there was barely enough space for even my stubby legs. I tried to imagine a tall European attempting to sit in seat number four, and figured that they would have had to work several years with Cirque du Soleil to manage the feat.

Somehow I wedged myself in. My feet were pigeon-toed and my knees tightly pressed together with my daypack on my lap. I looked up just in time to catch the baby being handed to me as a mother and her other two daughters debated the best way for them to tackle seat number three. The mother, who wore a colorful skirt, petticoats, and a black bowler hat, somehow managed to squeeze into that distressingly small space. The two daughters, aged seven and nine, plopped onto her lap. She smiled at me with a wonderful gap-toothed grin, but made no attempt to retrieve her baby I was holding at arm's length. Not that they had any room in seat number three.

Cautiously, I brought the newborn in for a closer look. Asleep in a bundle of old tattered towels, she had dark ebony hair that was plastered to her little round face, and her little fists opened and closed whenever I placed my finger in her grip.

I began to chat with the daughters, who spoke fluent Spanish. The mother knew only a little. They were a Quechua family, indigenous farmers from the region. The father was standing at the back of the bus, as they only had enough money to pay for the one seat.

This was their biannual trip to the city, where they would purchase their staples for the following months. They would buy sugar, flour, and some seeds for planting. The girls were very excited about the trip and had dressed in their best clothes; although they were faded and either too big or too small, I could tell that much care had been taken to clean and mend them.

We began talking about the Quechua culture. The girls did not attend school, as they were needed at home to work. They were very excited to teach me some of their traditional language, and had a good laugh at my accent. I pulled out a pen and notebook and began writing down some of the common phrases.

I had almost forgotten the baby I was holding until she suddenly became very awake. She reached up and yanked my hair, almost as if to ring the dinner bell. In a complicated shuffle resembling a game of Twister, I passed the baby to her mom and one of the girls came to sit on my lap while the baby was being fed. For most of the trip, the baby was a delight and rarely cried. As soon as she was happily full, I took her in my arms again.

As our journey continued, I shared tales of Canada and my own family, with the girls translating the parts their mother could not understand. The mother was shocked that I was traveling on my own, was still unmarried, and had no children, yet was almost an old lady at thirty!

Normally, a bus ride of eight hours in a horribly cramped seat would have been miserable and long, but this voyage became a memory to cherish. I grew sad as we reached our destination, knowing I would most likely never see my new friends again. We had shared stories and food, laughed at the baby's antics, and clutched one another whenever the bus reeled around a corner at breakneck speeds.

"Trrree-si-a." The mother repeated my name several times and motioned for my pen. She pulled the baby's arm from the bundle, pointed to the pen, then down at the baby's arm. One of the girls made it clear that I was to write my name on the arm. Did she want my autograph? I must have looked stunned, because the girls had to convince me that this was what the mother wanted. Once there was no doubt, I reached down and wrote my name in tiny block letters on the baby's pudgy little arm.

The mother seemed very pleased, and the daughters explained that she wanted to name the baby after me.

I was at a loss for words. During my travels I have often received gifts from people who own very little, yet they have insisted on sharing their few treasures with me. In this case they had nothing material to offer, so they gave me something invaluable, making me their daughter's namesake. It is moments like these when one is blessed with the true gift of traveling.

I often think about that lovely Quechua family and wonder about a little girl named "Trrreeesia" who lives in the Peruvian highlands. I hold that bus ride more dear to my heart than visiting Cuzco, Machu Pichuu, and the Nazca Lines. So the next time you have to make a choice between the luxury coach and the local hunk of junk, just think of the cultural pilgrimage you might miss out on. It's every traveler's rite of passage.

Tricia Duncan is a former nomadic raft guide who for fifteen years enjoyed tent living, van camping and couch surfing. She and her Kiwi husband, Royce Casford, recently settled in Paradise Valley, BC, where they purchased clothes hangers, silverware and a bed with legs for the first time ever! The new adventure of motherhood is about to begin for Tricia, which should make international travel look like a walk in the park.

Mekong King

Travel plans can be highly overrated.

By Steve Bramucci

While having dinner with some friends in Bangkok one evening, I finally revealed my plan—ill conceived and poorly formulated as it was. I had decided to buy a boat, several days' worth of food and clean water, and then row down the Mekong Delta from the Cambodia–Vietnam border all the way to Ho Chi Minh City at the river's mouth.

The Mekong is one of the world's mighty rivers. It trickles down from the Himalayas in Tibet, nourishing one of Asia's great rice growing regions in China, Cambodia, and Vietnam as it cuts a swath toward the South China Sea. The Mekong Delta is a confusing network of river channels in South Vietnam that covers forty thousand square kilometers—an area roughly the size of Switzerland.

Our friends Rudolpho and Ann, who once lived in Vietnam, got a big laugh out of my idea, and weren't exactly encouraging about my prospects. Katrin, my girlfriend, decided to pass on the Mekong trip in favor of a week at a Buddhist monastery. It was suggested at dinner that her decision proved she was already wiser than me.

And that's how I ended up—by myself—on a plane to Phnom Penh, Cambodia. While waiting on the tarmac for take-off, I had a short exchange with the couple sitting next to me.

"I am planning to buy a small boat and take it down the Mekong Delta alone," I said.

Laughter.

On the one-hour flight from Bangkok, the woman eventually suspended her disbelief over the absurdity of my plan. We settled into a conversation that ranged across many subjects. The man, on the other hand, was still chortling away when the plane landed. With sympathy in their eyes, they drove me to the waterfront in Phnom Penh and requested that, if I survived, I should contact them when the trip was over.

Down at the waterfront I pointed to a raft and asked the owner if it was for sale. This initial choice was not a good one. The raft, it turned out, was actually a mobile fish farm. Besides, the river was moving so slowly in that section that it probably would have taken me a month to reach my destination.

Instead, I caught a speedboat to Chau Doc, the first town of note on the Vietnamese side of the border. I bought some clay-pot fish for dinner, sauntered through town, and played with some kids who wanted to practice their English, then went to bed early.

I bought a boat the next morning. It was old, worn, and ratty looking. By my estimation, I paid the market price for an old, worn, and ratty boat ... plus a forty-percent mark-up, the requisite "tourist tax" charged to all visitors from foreign lands. The boat was about seven feet long and had a rowing platform on the back. Small skiffs like this are commonly used by women for short-distance transport on the canals, such as ferrying people from one side of a canal to the other. Even for an optimist like myself, travelling a hundred and sixty kilometers in my boat was a bold prospect. The well-worn bailing pan suggested it had been used a great deal.

I used a translator to negotiate the boat sale. The price stood at one hundred U.S. dollars and never budged, an unusual phenomenon in Southeast Asia. When I asked why the price wasn't flexible, the translator told me the woman selling the boat thought I was either crazy or eager to drown—neither of which led to a good bargaining position. I was satisfied by this answer and paid up. On the upside, I brought joy to the entire village: never had laughter echoed across the Mekong like it did when I divulged my plan. The consensus was that I wouldn't last a day, and certainly wouldn't make it out of Chau Doc. The hotel desk clerk said he would hold a room for me.

I bought enough bananas for a week, rope, a knife, a few candles, some cookies, and bait for fishing (though I had nothing to cook any fish with). I also had a copy of Huckleberry Finn and some patching putty for making simple repairs. I hopped in my boat—already carrying six inches of river water—and pushed off.

That was when I received the first major shock of the expedition: I was being pushed back upriver by the current, and I had no idea why. I was going with the flow, so to speak, but the flow was taking me back toward Cambodia. So I started looking for a canal to take me out to the big river—perhaps it would be flowing in the right direction.

Although I was being pushed in the wrong direction, there was plenty to see. Over the next few hours I passed bridges constructed with a single bamboo pole, slanting stilt houses, and Asian men fishing or swimming across the river with their water buffaloes. I created quite a scene whenever I passed a small village. Curious people would follow me along the shore until they tired of waiting for me to make forward progress. They would then yell "Hello!" five or six times (as is the custom there), and then go home.

While I paddled along, I contemplated possible names for my boat, and it only made sense that I should name mine after an important woman in my life, just like Forrest Gump had. Katrin was the obvious choice—or perhaps even my mother—but then I realized this wouldn't be flattery for either. I settled on The Duchess of Bilgewater, figuring this name would be more appropriate.

At dark, my little canal intersected with a big section of river and I arrived at a floating village. I pulled in to ask for directions and was offered a bed at the home of a fish farmer and his wife. We communicated by pointing to phrases in my English-Vietnamese guidebook. When I showed them *How do I get to Sa Dec* (a city 160 kilometers downriver), the fish farmer looked at me, momentarily bewildered, then called my attention to the Vietnamese word for car.

I laughed.

He pointed to the word for car again and kept a very straight face.

We had a nice dinner of fish with rice and tea. The Mekong rice is better than any other rice I've had, but I was hesitant to eat too much because it didn't seem like the family's larder was overflowing with excess. In exchange I passed cookies around for desert. When it was time for bed they arranged a mat for me, aligning it so I was facing various religious shrines, while ensuring I wouldn't roll into the large hole that occupied half of their floor (this is where the fish were raised). I slept quite well, considering waves frequently sloshed up from passing cargo boats.

I woke ten minutes before sunrise. It was one of the most picturesque sunrises I've ever seen: red and purple hues filled the sky as the riverbank slowly softened and came into focus. The village sprang to life the instant light appeared—the Mekong is characterized as being sleepy, but its people are not.

My hosts emphatically refused to accept money from me. Drawing a small map on a piece of paper, I indicated my quandary: "Which direction to Sa Dec?"

The man pointed back toward Chau Doc.

I asked again. I got the same answer.

This exchange went on for a couple of minutes until I pointed in the opposite direction of Chau Doc and said, "Sa Dec?" The man gave a half-hearted nod, which was good enough for me. After bailing the water that had collected in my boat, I hopped in and pushed into the river, waving as I went.

I paddled the canals all day, creating bigger stirs as I ventured further and further from places that are visited by tourists. When I landed in some of these locations, it was not uncommon for the local people to touch, pinch, and pet me. They said, "Hello," and I replied, "Thank you," using my best Vietnamese.

They often called to me from shore; a lot of the older women indicated they wanted to see me row using the traditional standing position, which of course I couldn't. In several places I saw huge fishing nets that were controlled by a lever arm, an ingenious invention. One man crossed the river using a zip line.

The Mekong is life to the canal people: they boil and drink the water, bathe in it, fish from it, and use it to irrigate their crops. Never have I seen people so connected to their environment.

By late afternoon I was making minimal progress again. Night was falling, so when a motorboat passed I tried hitching a ride. They stopped. I threw them a rope and they towed me as far as they were going. They enjoyed the novelty of it, and I was grateful for the lift. They invited me aboard and I shared my cookies in exchange for some rice and dried fish. The crew pointed me out to all passersby, showing them what the tide had brought in. There was a lot of wild-eyed laughter.

I managed to get two more lifts before reaching a small town. I was convinced no tourist had ever been there because I was gawked at like people would gawk at Angelina Jolie if she made an appearance at a municipal swimming pool. They bought me beers. I tried to figure out what town I was in, because it wasn't in my guidebook. I eventually realized the town was situated ninety kilometers north of Sa Dec and about a hundred and ten kilometers north of Vinh Long. I had been on the water for two days and I was still far from my destination—a crushing blow to my optimism.

*   *   *

Oh, the spectacle I made! I was a giant in Vietnam—not to mention white and blond. Anyone who wants attention—traffic-stopping attention—should forget about dieting, Botox, or Tae Bo. Go to the unvisited reaches of the Mekong.

Two men watched me curiously from a foot away while I wrote my sister a birthday email. That morning I had found two children waiting outside the hotel to further inspect me. The previous night a drunken man kept trying to get into my room. Fortunately the hotel staff, having seen the firm arms-length distance I had started keeping from villagers, understood that my personal visiting hours were over.

On my walk the next morning, I turned around and saw the entire bustling street behind me frozen and gawking. Truly, it was like a Capra movie—every single person was staring at me.

I sent an email to a Vietnamese friend back in the States, asking him to translate the following statement for me:

Hello! I am a traveler who has purchased a boat in Chau Doc. I am trying to get to Sa Dec, which may be impossible. Would you be interested in trading my boat for a used bicycle?

That's what I was thinking that morning. I hadn't heard back from my friend by noon, so I went to the dock to collect my boat. When I arrived at the dock I discovered that a woman had switched her oars with mine, but a little peer pressure from her neighbors and she reluctantly gave them back.

I have to be honest: I was rather enjoying my celebrity status. At a small café I was again swarmed by locals, and we all laughed over my general predicament. Then I waved goodbye and paddled out toward the big water.

It took me an hour to get into the middle of the river, but once I managed to get there, I felt great. The river was in front of me and the scenery on either side was classic Mekong imagery: fruit orchards, ramshackle homes, rice fields being plowed by water buffaloes. I decided to relax for an hour or so and enjoy. I swam, ate a few bananas, and tried to teach myself the upright rowing style. I wanted to see if I could figure it out, and found that it's a lot like self-propelled surfing. Once you learn, it feels more natural than backward rowing. When I managed to get in a rhythm, I glided.

Later that afternoon I spotted salvation in the form of a two-hundred-foot barge. I turned my boat and started rowing quickly in an attempt to cut it off. I rowed like a maniac. I caught the rhythm—*pull, turn down wrists, push, glide*. The barge was a mile away, behind me and to my right, but gaining fast. I set a line and went hard.

With a football field still between us, my legs were shaking and my arms were on fire. I had to keep my torrid pace—large boats don't turn off their engines to stop for small boats. I would have to cross its line.

I pushed myself hard—*pull, turn down wrists, push, glide*—and came to the barge just as it was motoring past me. Another ten seconds and I would have missed my chance. I held out my towline and the sailors took it and helped me aboard. There was plenty of shock when they found out what I was doing. They poked me in the ribs repeatedly, laughed, and led me around the barge on a tour.

I asked where they were going.

Ho Chi Minh City, they said.

Incredible. If I wanted I could push straight through with them. In the end, however, I decided to maintain a more leisurely pace. I told them I would ride as far as Sa Dec and put off there, which meant I would get to row around Sa Dec and Vinh Long—both cities I wanted to see—before continuing on to Ho Chi Minh.

And their boat? There wasn't anything more comfortable. I could sit on the side with my feet in the water, napping or peacefully watching the scenery pass by. I read Huck Finn and watched the sun set over the Mekong.

Once it was dark, the crew invited me to eat with them. We tried to communicate, but couldn't get beyond a few shared words. At night the mosquitoes feasted on the human buffet, the mites took a shot at cleanup, the flies hurried in for dessert, and the fleas licked the plate. At around midnight I felt the barge stop. The captain explained using hand gestures that the barge was grounded in shallow water.

After a time I understood. The Mekong is tidal. It's that big. Which is why my initial efforts to row downstream had taken me upstream instead—an effect akin to climbing the down escalator.

*   *   *

I woke up at five the next morning and decided to check on the Duchess. She was sunk, but her nose was tied to the barge and was still poking an inch out of the water. A rescue mission ensued. The crew tied ropes to her back and pulled her up on the anchor hoist of the barge. I bailed the water and began repairing. A few planks were lost, as were my knife and my drinking water. I used the last of my putty for patchwork, nailing some of the front planks to the back so that I could stand and row.

After the repair work, I spent the rest of the day lazing around, snacking on dried fish, and jumping off the roof of the grounded barge into the river. The barge continued chugging downriver when the tide rose later that afternoon. Not long after we resumed our journey, however, a violent storm rolled in.

Not everyone has witnessed a storm on the water, and now that I have, I'm in no rush for a repeat experience. It was truly wild. Lightning zigzagged across the sky and thunder exploded; there was no lag between the two. I shivered uncontrollably as I bailed the rapidly filling Duchess, trying to keep her afloat.

Then the captain sent a message back that we were coming to Sa Dec. My choices were to yawl off and try to make shore mid-storm, in which case I could be warm in an hour. Or I could skip Sa Dec for Vinh Long and yawl off in two hours, when guesthouses would be closing and people would be heading to bed.

Worried that we'd be following the storm downriver, I decided to risk paddling for Sa Dec in the electrical storm. The second the line was untied from the barge, I regretted my choice; I was at least a mile from shore and rowing was almost impossible with the huge waves sloshing over the sides of my skiff. I could take only two or three strokes with the oars before having to jump to the bottom of the skiff and bail. My backpack started to float on the growing pool in the boat. The sky was pitch black, except for those moments when lightning made the rain sparkle like falling diamonds. I was tossed from side to side and turned around in circles, out of control. All I could do was keep rowing.

After an hour of fanatical rowing, I watched with relief as the storm passed and the sky cleared. Soon I saw a small dock with a family huddled under a tin roof. In their eyes I saw shock; in my eyes they saw that I needed a warm, dry place to sleep. The family had a friend nearby who spoke some English and soon they had agreed to keep The Duchess safe for the night. Then the eldest son gave me a ride on the back of his motorcycle into town, dropping me off at a huge, empty war-era hotel.

The next day I gave my boat to a fish farmer. He was not impressed. Somewhere in the storm, my notion of rowing all the way to Ho Chi Minh had vanished. While I didn't make it to the river's mouth, I did travel more than a hundred and fifty kilometers down the Mekong Delta, visiting hidden villages that don't appear on maps, living with the crew of a barge, and braving a wild storm.

I guess you can say it worked out exactly like I had planned.

*Steve Bramucci is a naturalist, adventurer, and travel writer who feels more at home on the floor of a floating fish farm than in a posh hotel. He can be reached at **stevebram@hotmail.com**.*

Trial by Thumb

Those were the days when we were young and lacked common sense.

By Rod Keays

My friend Larry and I were fresh out of high school and we couldn't wait to leave town. Young people were hitting the highway in droves back in the 1970s—venturing off to see North America with their backpacks and thumbs. We were both nineteen and had planned our trip across Canada for about three days, which we figured was good enough. I forget how much money Larry had, but I only had ninety dollars.

"No problem," I told Larry. "It's summer. We'll get jobs picking fruit in the Okanagan Valley. They always need pickers at this time of year."

Our first ride took us all the way from Vancouver to Hope, BC, a small mountain town a hundred and fifty kilometers inland from the Pacific. It's where the Hope-Princeton Highway begins, and at that time was the only route east other than the Trans-Canada Highway, which follows the Fraser Canyon north and west to Kamloops.

From earlier trips around Vancouver we had learned the hitchhiker's Number One Rule: when choosing a place to hitch a ride, make sure there's enough room for a car to pull off the road. If there isn't, it can be hazardous to other motorists. Having room to pull over also gives you the chance to take a good look at the driver and other passengers before getting inside their vehicle. If they look like boozers or rednecks—potential threats to your life—you can always decline the ride.

Rule Number Two is to make sure there's nobody else hitching in the same spot. On the outskirts of Hope we found at least ten groups of hitchhikers, so we had to get in line and wait for all of them to get rides before we could stick out our thumbs. We learned quickly that hitchhikers can be fiercely territorial; if we so much as stuck out a pinky at the back of the queue, we got shouted down. For this reason, it was hours before we got a ride out of Hope.

We reached the Okanagan with high hopes of swimming and meeting some girls. Girls were the best way to get rides. I can still recall the first time I hitched with a girl; she told me to hide in the trees by the side of the road and then lifted her skirt to show some leg. The first car stopped a few seconds later. Talk about friendly!

When Larry and I reached Vernon we found the swimming was great, but there weren't any girls who had eyes for us. We did manage to land a job picking fruit, however. It was a rite of passage for teens in western Canada to do this at least once. We worked hard for three days straight and slept inside a small pickers' cabin in the orchard. On the final day we cashed out. We made far less than we had hoped, partly because Larry ate much of what he'd picked. He even fell off the pickers' ladder a couple of times, so he started climbing the trees instead. He also refused to pick the apples with their stems on, which made the owner angry.

I was glad to move on.

At the outskirts of Vernon we chose what appeared to be a good hitchhiking spot at the roadside. I walked over to a highway sign to take off my backpack ... and nearly stepped on a rattlesnake, coiled on the asphalt warming itself in the sun. It rattled its tail. With my heart in my throat, I slowly backed away.

The next day we reached the wide-open grasslands and vistas of Alberta, its wheat fields sprawling as far as the eye could see. We were dropped off in Edmonton, which to us looked like a working-class city with mean-faced men on the streets. We were tired and dirty from the trip through the Rockies, and were looking forward to cleaning up and eating something. But finding a hostel was not as easy as we'd hoped. Eventually, a bus driver gave us directions to the hostel and everything started to feel better.

We had just showered and were starting to get settled in the hostel when several large fellows appeared in our room. The leader was a short, muscular, sour-faced man with stringy black hair hanging below his shoulders. He started yelling at me and demanding his money. When I tried to explain that I didn't know what he was talking about, he got more and more agitated. His friends formed a circle around me. Suddenly, he drew a knife and threw it. I could feel the displaced air as the blade whistled between my legs, and with an overwhelmingly loud *Twwoonngggg!* it stuck into the floorboards behind me.

Thankfully, this exhausted his anger somewhat, and I got my chance to figure out what was going on. It turned out that the person who had occupied the bunk before me had permanently "borrowed" some hash from this fellow. The victim had never seen the thief, but he knew which bunk he'd been sleeping in, and that bunk just happened to be mine. He had therefore assumed I was the thief.

I wasn't hurt, but that was enough of Edmonton for us.

The next day we hitched south to Calgary and promptly got stuck in town. Nobody would stop for us, so eventually we had to take a bus to a junction outside the city. We found a suitable spot in the shade and stuck out our thumbs. Half an hour later, a passing pickup truck pulled over, drove over our backpacks, and kept on going.

An hour after that, another pickup truck stopped at a farmhouse near where we were sitting. Ten minutes later they drove out of the driveway, and as they passed, they slowed down and threw two bags of garbage at us. Do you remember my earlier comment about not accepting rides with rednecks? Believe me, it was for your own safety.

We finally managed a ride to Medicine Hat, a quiet little town with clean streets and a calm attitude. People there seemed friendly—and we sure needed a rest. We stayed at the hostel for as long as possible; our nerves were still shaken by the knife incident and we were getting tired of the long waits for rides. After four days they kicked us out, and on a hot, bright, and sunny morning we started walking east along the Trans-Canada Highway, thumbing as we went.

We walked and walked and walked; we drank our water and ate our food until it was gone. We had started walking at eight a.m., and at sunset we still hadn't been picked up. By this time we were a long way from town. There were so few cars on the road and so few lights that it felt like we were alone on Earth. We started to worry that we might get stranded at the side of the road.

Then, near the horizon, I saw something moving. I turned on my flashlight and the beam reflected off something. It came closer, appearing and disappearing behind hills and bushes as it moved. It grew bigger and bigger, and then suddenly ... the sound of a screaming baby filled our ears!

No. Not a baby. It was some kind of wild animal.

Larry and I realized we were about to have a confrontation. I had a Swiss Army knife; Larry pulled out the tent poles. We were shaking with fear when it appeared on the far side of the road, only a few meters away: a bobcat, snarling and spitting at us.

We were terrified, but we held our ground. We shouted at it and made striking motions with our weapons. It hesitated long enough for us to run into the middle of the highway and flag down a transport truck. He screeched to a halt and reluctantly let us inside.

When we told him the story, he didn't even believe us. In fact, we must have said something to piss him off because a few kilometers down the road he almost booted us out of the truck. But he didn't. The three of us sat in silence all the way to Regina.

(Three years later, by chance, I was living in Regina, where I met a wildlife biologist. He told me the bobcat was probably rabid, and we were very fortunate not to have been attacked. He said it was extremely rare for a cat to behave in that manner unless it was sick or starving.)

When we reached Ontario, life on the road settled down to a boring itinerary of long waits and blackflies. One night in a tent at Lake of the Woods campground convinced me to stay out of Ontario in the summer. While sleeping, I leaned one of my arms against the tent wall and the bloody insects bit me right through the canvas, leaving huge welts all over my elbow. The blighters!

The next day, a transport truck with a livestock trailer pulled over. The driver got out of the truck with a big grin on his face and asked where we were going.

"Toronto," I said.

He led us around to the back of the pig trailer and opened the doors. "In there?" I asked, disbelieving. But we soon understood. There were thirty other hitchhikers inside the trailer, and they shouted at us to pass up our gear. There were no pigs on board.

The trailer had several inches of fresh straw and was partitioned off into sections that measured about six feet by four feet. I was looking forward to getting some sleep, but it was not to be. The trucker drove all night; in the trailer everyone was playing guitars, singing, drinking beer, and smoking cigarettes. The driver made it to Toronto the next morning, and by this time we were all hungry, sore, and bleary-eyed. But the driver seemed to have that same smile on his face. Larry and I sauntered off to the nearest cafe for a big cup of coffee and breakfast.

The journey home was sure a lot easier. Larry and I anted up and purchased train tickets all the way back to Vancouver. No more hitchhiking for us!

Rod Keays discovered writing as a teenager while playing bass guitar in a Rock and Roll band called Misty Daze. He wrote romantic poetry with the lead singer, which they turned into songs. Now he writes travel stories that involve episodes of getting beaten up, being dumped by gorgeous women, and living in a run down cabin on Salt Spring Island. Writing, he says, helps to keep those memories fresh and alive. He lives in Victoria, BC, where he now works as a gardener and landscaper.

Foraging

Life in the Amazon Jungle is far from routine.

By Jamella Hagen

En bolsa?" asked the weathered-looking woman behind the counter of the crowded restaurant. She dipped a ladle into a cauldron of hot chicken vegetable soup.

"Si?" I guessed. My Spanish was poor to begin with, and in the Peruvian jungle the local dialect was nearly impossible for me to understand. I knew that *bolsa* means bag, so I assumed she was talking about takeout.

My stomach rumbled. My partner Justin was waiting outside in a taxi. We were on our way to the Picaflor Research Center on the Tambopata River, which is at the headwaters of the Amazon, a place where wild jaguars still prowl the undergrowth. The isolated research station is run by an Anglo-Peruvian couple—she a biologist, he a boat driver—who partially fund their research by accommodating working volunteers in exchange for reasonably priced food and lodging.

Justin and I had discovered the research station while searching the Internet for affordable jungle adventures, and were so thrilled by the prospect that we went immediately to an electronics market in Cusco to book our stay. Over a crackly radiophone, our host

Laurel warned us that getting to Picaflor would be part of the adventure. She tried to help by giving directions.

"You'll have to cross a *football pitch*," she said through the static.

"You're breaking up," I told her. "But we'll be sure to look for the *footbridge*."

We flew to the tiny town of Puerto Maldonado and were immediately confronted with the challenge of finding a taxi willing to drive us to the old port where we would meet the Picaflor supply boat. The research station was accessible only by watercraft, a five-hour trip upriver.

We eventually found a willing driver, but we were already behind schedule, and the situation only grew worse when he stopped for gas, then to ask for directions, and finally to pick up some lunch. We were both famished ourselves, so instead of arguing with the driver, I decided to go inside and order some food.

The woman behind the counter poured a ladleful of steaming soup straight into a thin plastic bag—the kind of bag North Americans use in the produce sections of our supermarkets. She tied the end of the bag in a knot to secure it, then held it out to me. I had to hold the bag near the top to avoid burning my fingers, and frankly, I was terrified the soup would melt through the bag and spill all over my lap the moment I sat down with it in the taxi. But the woman and the taxi driver seemed to think it was normal, so I paid up and left.

Our driver turned down a one-lane track through the forest and followed it until the road ended at a soccer field. Surrounding us was a small country village of the kind we'd become accustomed to seeing in Peru—small family dwellings with pigs and chickens milling about. The driver put up his hands and shrugged. He didn't know where to go. There was no sign of a port or a footbridge. He asked a local for directions, then rolled his eyes and continued along an even narrower dirt track until we came to a small clearing in the jungle. Ahead of us was the wide, muddy Tambopata River.

The driver shrugged again, indicating that this was as far as he could possibly go, then motioned for us to get out. We hauled our backpacks out of the trunk while a couple of interested locals observed us from a safe distance. Hot, hungry, and late for our rendezvous with the Picaflor supply boat, we watched the taxi disappear into the trees, then turned to the observers for advice.

"You want Roberto," they told us. "He left ten minutes ago." Ten minutes ago sounded about right, but I had never heard of anybody named Roberto.

Two women flagged down a motorized canoe for us, which we presumed would take us to Roberto. We got in and the boatman pushed off from shore. We were already past the midstream point when we saw a pair of frantic arms waving at us from the shoreline we'd just left. Our canoe driver expressed frustration when we asked him to turn back, but he did so anyway. When we got back to shore, a short and extremely muscular Peruvian man was laughing and gesturing toward us.

"Picaflor?" I asked hopefully.

"Si, si," he said. "Gayella? Guillermo?"

"Jamella," I said, relieved. It was pretty close to my name.

He introduced himself as Pico, explaining that he and Laurel would be our hosts at Picaflor. We followed Pico as he hefted a jerry can full of gasoline in each hand and headed down the slippery bank, his biceps rippling. After loading our bags onto the boat, we helped load provisions of fruit, vegetables, and flour.

As we started up the river, I turned to the bags of takeout soup I'd purchased from the little restaurant along the way. I offered some to Pico, saying, "Sorry, we haven't got spoons."

Pico roared with laughter. "*Somos en la selva,*" he explained: "We're in the jungle now." He dipped a muscular hand into the steaming soup and ate with relish. We did the same.

*   *   *

Justin and I consider ourselves adventurous; before braving the jungle we'd done several hikes in the Peruvian Andes. Still, when our hosts Pico and Laurel announced they were going into town, I must admit I felt apprehensive at spending a night by ourselves in the jungle.

For me, the jungle seemed like a dangerous place—the kind of place where things you don't know about can kill you in 3.5 seconds or less. Since our arrival with Pico, we'd had two days to explore the jungle surrounding the research station. We had learned why it would not be prudent to swim in the river: Pico pointed out the resident black caiman—a crocodilian creature that can reach up to four meters in length. There was also the deadly green vine snake Justin spotted in a tree; bullet ants (so named because if they sting you, it feels like you've been shot); and the mother tarantula Pico had taken great delight in showing us. The giant spider lived next to the water pump—her body, including the legs, was as large as my hand.

The human element made us a little nervous, too. Pico and Laurel seemed overly eager to have us house-sit, explaining that things had gone missing a few times when they'd left the place unattended. The day before their departure, Laurel had also taken us out to document illegal logging on the property. While we hadn't run into the bandits themselves, we'd heard the eerie drone of their chainsaws in the distance. One of the things Laurel planned to do while in town was develop the photographs and turn them over to the police. What if these people knew we'd been taking pictures of their illegal activities for the authorities? Had we left behind any traces?

Nevertheless, the idea of an "unsupervised" overnight stay in the jungle was also a thrill, so we agreed to man the radiophone and watch the house—which was really just a series of screened-in porches covered with palm thatch.

"Don't worry," Laurel assured us. "We'll be home tomorrow evening."

Justin and I listened to the drone of the canoe's engine until it faded out of earshot, then started attending to our most basic needs: we headed for the kitchen to round up some dinner. There seemed to be plenty of food—buckets and jars full of provisions— but nothing ready to eat. Feeling rather primal, we changed tactics and went outside to an area Laurel described as "the garden" to see if we could find something fresh.

The garden was indistinguishable from the surrounding jungle, but we did find a banana tree with a bundle of bananas that looked ripe. The only question was how to get them down.

"Can you climb the tree?" I asked Justin. I was secretly hoping he would play the role of manly provider.

"The tree doesn't look strong enough," he said. "Do you think we can knock them down with a stick?"

"I think we'd need a machete to cut through the stem," I said. "But we'll have to reach it first." Machete wielding was a skill we'd picked up over the last two days, and I already liked to pretend that I knew what I was talking about.

Stymied, we moved on to a papaya tree, which had one beautiful ripe fruit hanging high above our heads. Justin and I took turns nudging at it with a long stick until one of us landed a blow that knocked down the sought-after fruit. That's when we discovered our beautiful papaya had already been eaten by birds—it was completely hollowed out on the side we couldn't see.

A jungle lesson: food must be shared around.

We eventually found some small red chili peppers growing in the garden, which we decided to combine with the canned beans and tomatoes we'd found inside. There was also flour and oil, so while I worked on a large pot of chili, Justin surprised me by revealing a hidden talent for baking bread.

In the jungle, inside and outside are not fixed boundaries. At bedtime, Justin and I walked into our room and found a gecko on the inside of the screen, devouring a moth. As we fell asleep, we were awakened by the harsh, barking cry of a bamboo rat, directly on the other side of the mesh. We shone our flashlights out and saw a brown, furry animal about the size of a small cat, its eye reflecting the light back at us.

We were wakened again later by a thunderstorm that shook the thin walls, then misted us with rain that filtered in through the screens. We thought of the enormous castaña (Brazil nut) trees above us on the hill and prayed the lightning was further away than it sounded.

The next morning dawned humid and calm. We'd been warned not to venture into the jungle on our own, but that didn't stop Justin from going for his morning "monkey walk." A family of saddleback tamarins showed up predictably each morning in a thicket of bamboo up the hill, and Justin used them as an excuse to go looking for what he really wanted to see—a jaguar. More nervous than excited by the possibility of encountering a large cat, I chose to stay and fulfill our house-sitting duties: pumping water and turning on the radiophone for the designated half-hour. To my surprise, I heard Laurel's voice come crackling over the speakers.

"The canoe's broken down," she explained. "We're stuck here until we can get it fixed—probably a couple more days. Is everything all right?"

Was everything all right? It seemed to be. A rash I'd noticed on my abdomen had flared up a little, but it didn't seem to require hospitalization as of yet.

"How do you harvest bananas?" I asked her.

"Sorry?"

"The bananas in your garden are ripe. How do we get them down?"

"Oh, you have to cut down the entire tree," she explained. "But be very careful with the machete."

The surrounding jungle always came alive at night. We became acutely aware of the forest and our presence in it, as if the screens on the upper halves of the walls at Picaflor had disappeared. To distract ourselves, we started venturing out on the boardwalk by the river, searching by flashlight for the eyes of caiman in the dark. One evening we found a family of pacas—mammals about the size of cocker spaniels, but with the spotted coats of young white-tailed deer. We watched as they ate what looked like fallen oranges from a tree near the house. What a good idea! We decided to try the oranges ourselves, only to find they were lemons in disguise.

As wild victuals continued to resist our approaches, we began to spend more time in the kitchen, turning to comfort food. A dusty bag of potatoes became golden French fries, while cans of olives and tuna blended with harvested chili peppers to create a deliciously spicy pasta sauce. Our most exciting ingredient, however, was the enormous bag of Brazil nuts, locally called castañas, sitting on the porch. The shells were hard and we spent hours cracking them open with a hammer. Our first attempts were disappointing—in the humid environment of the jungle, many of the nuts had decayed into a powder of blue mould. But as we persisted, our selection skills improved and eventually we had a pile of nuts that we combined with pancakes, banana bread, and my personal favorite—chewy oatmeal cookies.

Of course, the more food we made, the more the jungle's residents came inside looking for a handout. Any bread we baked had to be eaten quickly—otherwise it would fill with a species of tiny red ant, even if kept in a tightly sealed box on the counter. All food had to be stored in sealed buckets to deter the rat that scampered through the rafters after dusk. And everything from snacks to clothing had to be carefully covered to keep it safe from the scattering of gecko feces that fell from the ceiling.

As for the bananas that Justin eventually harvested from the garden and hung on the porch, they were the most sought-after item of all. This was a lesson I learned on a nighttime trip down the open-air walkway to the bathroom. As I shuffled along, half asleep, something swooped down from above and brushed against my hair. I'm not usually the type to shriek, but I was so startled that I shrieked long, loud, and clear.

Justin came tearing down the hall to find me shrieking at a small, harmless fruit bat that was swooping again and again at the hanging bananas. The next night we discovered a porcupine on the porch trying to get at them; the night after that, Justin found an opossum clinging to the yellow cluster. We did manage to eat a few of the prized bananas ourselves, but those that were split open had to be abandoned to the bees, beetles, wasps, and ants who came to polish off the remains.

When Pico and Laurel finally returned from Puerto Maldonado, a full five days had passed. They brought with them two new volunteers, and the jungle house filled with activity once again. We shared our small mountain of baked goods and our stories of pacas, porcupines, and two men who had appeared on the porch one morning—knives in hand—asking our permission to harvest leaves from the riverbank.

It was nice to have the company again, but we were also a little sorry to lose our solitary jungle retreat. In the end, we'd come to feel remarkably at home under the thatch and bamboo on the crowded banks of the Tambopata.

Jamella Hagen is making her first foray into travel writing after realizing there is no money in poetry. You'll often find her hiking on mountain trails around the world—though just as often she may be lost and searching for the trail. Jamella, whose nonfiction articles have appeared in Okanagan Life, *recently completed an MFA in Creative Writing at UBC. One of her nonfiction articles was also shortlisted for a CBC Literary Award in 2007.*

African Rhythm

Sometimes you need a little faith ... and a few wits ...
and a bit of luck.

By Jennifer Braun

"Get in!" said the Afrikaner man driving the *bakkie*. "What are you girls doing out here? You could get yourselves killed!"

This was not the first time we had received a tongue-lashing from a white African in a truck. Like many people we'd met—including our parents—he figured that two North American girls hitchhiking through southern Africa must either be ignorant or have some kind of death wish. Then there were those white people—often driving BMWs and Mercedes—who would slow down, stare at us as they passed, and then speed up again as though we had some kind of contagious disease.

Rickety cars driven by black Africans stopped more often, their vehicles held together with what could only be pure faith. Usually there were already more people than seats, so we would respectfully decline. This usually elicited an "Ah! It's no problem!" from the driver, and they would figure out a way to shoehorn us inside.

Despite the stereotypes, over the three weeks my girlfriend Carey and I spent thumbing our way around several south African countries, we met a plethora of wonderful people—black and white alike.

*   *   *

In 1997, with a desire to contribute something meaningful to this world, I traveled to Africa from Canada to spend a year doing volunteer work. An organization called World Teach placed me in an unpaid teaching position in Sibasa, South Africa, where I helped high school students with their English. I also helped to computerize the library, and worked with other faculty members to write a play.

During my time off, I noticed that people often relied on hitchhiking as a means of transportation, particularly in the rural areas. It was cheaper—and often more reliable—than taxis or buses. In fact, hitchhiking was so common that, several months into my sojourn, I began to plot a hitchhiking adventure with another volunteer, an American girl named Carey. We planned to thumb our way north to the border and then continue through neighboring Zimbabwe, Zambia, and Botswana for our first holiday. Having been schooled in a Western style of organization, we carefully planned our three-week trip and faxed a copy of our itinerary to our parents back home.

After spending our first night with some friends near the South Africa–Zimbabwe border, about 150 kilometers north of Sibasa, Carey and I walked across to Beitbridge, Zimbabwe. From Beitbridge there were two roads: one going northwest to Bulawayo, the other going northeast to Harare. A few people stopped and said they could take us into Harare for a "Good price!" Carey and I declined as politely as possible, as we were intent on hitchhiking to Bulawayo, about five hours away.

To speed up the process, Carey pulled out some paper to make a sign that said BULAWAYO. Just then, a shiny green *bakkie* (a small pickup truck) pulled over. A handsome young English Zimbabwean rolled down his window and asked, "Where are you ladies off to?"

"Bulawayo," we said, shading our eyes from the sun.

"Shame. I'm going to Harare."

Carey and I looked at each other, then back at him. In a split second we telepathically communicated and in unison exclaimed, "Okay, we'll go to Harare then!"

We threw our mammoth backpacks into the back of his truck and, ditching the schedule we had spent hours on, set off to find adventure in Africa.

We became fast friends with the driver, a twenty-four-year-old businessman named Duncan. He worked for Hugo International, a firm based out of Johannesburg, training black Africans for jobs in communications. Duncan was refreshing because he was one of the first white Africans we'd met who did not have racist tendencies. He was on his way back to Harare to visit his parents.

Duncan drove for half an hour before stopping and treating us to lunch at a restaurant with a thatched roof and big game on the menu. After eating, we continued north toward Harare until a violent thunderstorm moved in. We stopped and pulled a tarp over our packs before they got soaked. Perhaps inspired by the poor weather, Duncan asked, "So where are you girls staying in Harare?"

"Oh, we'll probably just stay at a campground or a hostel," I said.

Sensing that we had no real plan, Duncan asked, "Would you like to stay with me and my family instead?"

Carey and I looked at each other again, almost disbelieving. "Okay!" we exclaimed.

We reached his parents' house about six hours later, and the Woods welcomed us as if we'd known them for years. We went out for dinner—their treat—and returned home at three a.m. after much food and drink.

The next morning we woke up at seven to Mrs. Wood's oatcakes for breakfast, and then Mr. Wood took us on a tour of his enormous bird sanctuary. Later still, Duncan treated us to a tour of the area. We saw elephants, ostriches, and other wild animals at a game reserve; admired Bushmen art at a geological wonder called the Balancing Rocks; and went for a swim at the idyllic Cleveland Dam.

In all, we stayed with Duncan and his family for three days, enjoying more excursions in and around Harare. We drank real coffee, ate our first pizza since coming to Africa, and bartered for textiles and carvings at the well-known Mbare market. Carey and Duncan even wound up sharing a few kisses.

*   *   *

From Harare we hitchhiked east toward Nyanga, a resort area in eastern Zimbabwe that sits on the border with Mozambique. After our serendipitous experience with Duncan and his parents, we adopted a new *laissez-faire* travel itinerary, taking the time to stop and see the sights along the way. We grew adept at hitchhiking, relying heavily on the fact we were friendly, foreign, and female to get us rides.

We managed to get a few rides in the back of pickups, sometimes jetting along at up to 170 kilometers an hour. The force of the wind flattened our sun-streaked hair to our faces, twirling it into small cyclones. Our lips tingled from the force of the wind, our teeth chattered, and my long purple skirt flapped like a sail. All of this while the gravel crunched under tires and the scenery wafted by, a blur of lollipop trees and green mountains juxtaposed against the blue-and-white sky. We passed lumbering elephants and laughing children, running and waving at us from the side of the road.

Sometimes people who picked us up were quiet and we would drive in silence, watching the African landscape change from sandy deserts to lush forests to bustling city streets. More often, people were chatty; they offered us pop or beer (I eventually got used to the driver drinking along with us), or food like *biltong* (dried meat) or sandwiches.

Always, people would ask the same question: "So, what do you think of our country?"

"Oh, it's a beautiful country," one of us would say, to which the other would invariably add, "Yes, and the people are so kind!"

Everybody likes to believe their country is the best in the world, so our comments would always bring a smile to the face of the driver.

Often, we'd then get a second question: "How does it compare to your country?"

A simple enough question, perhaps, but having been privileged with a North American lifestyle, we were always careful with our response.

"Well, in some ways it's quite different," we'd say. "For example, it's much colder where we live. But in other ways, it's the same. People want a family, a job, and a house."

We didn't mention the massive beehive teeming with bees that we had found inside our dilapidated bathroom cupboard in Sibasa, or that we'd had no hot water during the coldest month, in spite of our daily calls to have it fixed. We didn't mention that things, in general, took much longer to get done, or sometimes didn't get done at all. Instead, we focused on the positive differences—that the average African was probably friendlier and more generous than the average North American. Or that the pace of living was much more relaxed than in Canada and the United States. We talked about how people in Africa laughed more, and sang and danced in the streets more, and that we loved seeing teenage boys walking with their arms wrapped around each other's shoulders.

We wanted people to know how grateful we were to be visitors in their beautiful countries, so we also steered away from politically contentious topics like race relations or the future of post-apartheid South Africa.

One of the most wonderful things about hitchhiking is its randomness. At one point Carey and I were on our way from Kasane (known as "the Four Corners," where Botswana meets Zambia, Zimbabwe, and Namibia) toward Francistown. A tour bus pulled over and inside we found a boisterous Botswana rugby team. They gave us a good-natured (if slightly lecherous) cheer as we boarded the bus, but they were nice enough guys. They were drinking beer (lots of it), singing classic rugby songs, and enjoying their trip immensely. At one point Carey and I carried on a conversation with one of the players, who was completely naked.

They eventually dropped us off at the St. Claire Lion Park, fourteen kilometers from Francistown, where we were kept awake all night by nearby lions copulating every fifteen minutes. It *was* mating season, after all.

Hitchhiking was always exciting, and we did have some harrowing experiences. Sometimes we had to wait for hours to get a lift, like in sparsely populated Namibia and Botswana, each of which has fewer than two million inhabitants. At other times we endured extreme heat or pouring rain. On a few occasions we had to give up and pay for a ride, which was a blow to our hitchhiking egos. Then there was the time we got distracted by a great conversation with a father and son and were dropped off outside Soweto, one of the most dangerous districts in Johannesburg. Two policemen picked us up and, after chastising us for our stupidity, drove us to safety.

There was one time that we genuinely feared for our lives. Carey and I blame ourselves for this because we broke our Number One Hitchhiking Rule: we ignored our gut instinct that told us not to take the ride.

It was getting late in the day and we were anxious to get to our destination. A truck stopped, driven by a Zimbabwean man named Joe who was accompanied by his friend from Bangladesh. We didn't discuss the ride before getting into the truck, thereby breaking our Number Two Rule. And I sat with Joe while Carey slid into the back with his friend—breaking our Number Three Rule, which was to never split up.

Joe had assured us they were going to Nyanga, but when he pulled back onto the road he started driving in the opposite direction. They told us they wanted to bring us to a casino in Chimanimani. After about an hour of traveling on an increasingly desolate road, passing dilapidated houses and sketchy-looking *shebeens* (unlicensed drinking establishments), I asked Joe to stop at a convenience store for a drink.

Carey and I got out of the truck and slowly made our way over to each other, trying to look casual as we walked into the store.

"Where the hell are we?" I said to Carey in a low voice as we paid for our Fantas. "This is not the way to Nyanga."

"I know," she replied. "And that idiot keeps saying 'I love you' and trying to put his arm around me."

We kept a watchful eye on the men outside, who were standing by the truck drinking Cokes and smoking.

"Are you serious? Joe keeps trying to hold my hand!"

"We gotta get out of here."

We somehow managed to convince Joe to turn around and drive back toward Nyanga. At Mutare, the next major town, we jumped out of the *bakkie*, grabbed our backpacks, and started to run, calling, "Thanks for the ride!" We quickly consulted our *Lonely Planet* guidebook, found the nearest phone, and we were soon whisked away by a friendly local named Sonya to an old barn that had been converted into a hostel.

Whether it was divine intervention or sheer luck, Carey and I emerged from this and other sketchy situations with the help of strangers like Sonya ... or Nicholas and Shane, two young fellows who rescued us from a pair of middle-aged Afrikaner men with dubious intentions.

Bossie and Stefan had seemed nice at first, and had taken us on a personalized tour of the Eastern Transvaal. We toured the Echo Caves with them (a geologist's stalactite dream), and stopped at various curio markets and a store in the shape of a large shoe. While Bossie remained harmless, Stefan became pathetic; he bragged about how rich he was and "accidentally" touched Carey's backside twice. Even though he had a daughter only a year younger than us, he kept trying to persuade us to go to a hotel so we could "party."

When we reached a place called God's Corner, Carey and I saw two young guys standing on the street corner. "Hey Jen, aren't those Andy's friends?" Carey asked me. She was communicating with me telepathically again.

"Oh, yeah, that's right!" I replied. "They live near here!" I tried to sound as natural as I could. "We better go over and say hello."

We walked up to the boys, who must have sensed that something was wrong because they played right along. We were complete strangers, of course, but we all pretended that we knew each other. We turned to Bossie and Stefan with a shrug and said, "Thanks for the ride!" And then we grabbed our packs and climbed into Shane's silver Volkswagen.

Nicholas and Shane drove us to Bourke's Luck Potholes, a series of dark pools and cylindrical rocks that have been formed by whirling water. Then they brought us to Blyde River Canyon, which is the world's third largest canyon and is frequently ranked as one of the most breathtaking sights in Africa. After a spectacular day of hiking—during which we encountered a black mamba and a family of barking baboons—Nicholas and Shane agreed to drive us to a nearby campground.

Just as we were leaving the canyon, however, their alternator broke. It was late in the day and there were no repair shops open, so we had to turn around and stay with their friends Malcolm and Nina, two guides who worked at the canyon. The six of us clicked so well that Carey and I stayed with them for the next two days and visited some other fascinating geological sites: God's Window, Pilgrim's Rest, and the Pinnacle. We spent each night playing games, having *braiis* (African barbecues), and talking and dancing into the early morning.

Once again, serendipity had quashed our original plans, only to reveal new friends and opportunities moments later. Proof positive that our smiles and upturned thumbs were the surest guides to another African adventure.

Jennifer Braun was born in the African country that's now known as Zambia, and she credits her parents with instilling in her a love of travel and adventure. After living in more than six countries, this self-proclaimed nomad has managed to lay down roots in Vancouver—thanks to her husband Dave, her amazing friends, and her love for teaching English and Writing to high school students.

Do you have a Great Story?

If you enjoyed this collection of stories and feel you have an outrageous, funny, heartwarming or inspirational tale that you would like to share, we would love to hear from you. Our only rules are that your story has to have some unusual, illuminating or humorous twist to it, that it's a true anecdote, and that it has something to do with travel or the Great Outdoors.

We are already working on a follow-up to *I Learned Kung Fu from a Bear Cub* and we are willing to look at either story proposals or pieces that have already been written. You don't have to be a professional writer. We look forward to hearing from anybody that has a great yarn to spin.

To obtain more detailed submission guidelines, please visit Summit Studios on our web site at:

www.summitstudios.biz

Please submit stories or story proposals by e-mail, fax, or snail mail to:

SUMMIT STUDIOS
#105, 2572 Birch St.
Vancouver, BC V6H 2T4
Fax: (778) 371-8561

E-mail: submissions@summitstudios.biz

We look forward to hearing from you.

Acknowledgements

A very special thanks to my wife, Stacey, who shares my passion for travel and the outdoors. She also shares my love for great stories. Without her unconditional support and her belief in my dream to found a publishing company, it would not have been possible to share these stories with you.

A big thanks to Curtis Foreman for his help with the editing and to Kirk Seton for a fantastic book design. They are both top-notch professionals.

Thanks to Ron Niebrugge for the great cover image of the kung fu bear cubs.

Thanks to my friends and family members who have offered their ideas, support, and critical feedback as this book has taken shape.

And finally, thanks to the many travelers who have contributed their stories to this book. Their willingness to share means that we're all a little richer.

Other Titles by Matt Jackson

Mugged by a Moose

Edited by Matt Jackson

Is a bad day spent outside really better than a good day at the office? This collection of twenty-three short stories aims to answer that question.

Humor/Travel • Softcover • 216 pages
$19.95 • ISBN 0973467134

"It's like Chicken Soup for the Funny Bone."
- The Kitchener-Waterloo Record

A Beaver is Eating My Canoe

Edited by Matt Jackson

Another collection of wacky, funny, and inspiring tales from the far side of beyond, written by twenty-five free-spirited wanderers.

Humor/Travel • Softcover • 224 pages
$19.95 • ISBN 9780973467161

The Canada Chronicles:
A Four-year Hitchhiking Odyssey

Written by Matt Jackson

Join the author on a four-year hitchhiking journey across Canada as he logs almost 30,000 kilometers, takes more than 25,000 photographs and meets hundreds of interesting characters from every corner of the country.

Adventure/Travel • Softcover
384 pages • 60 color photographs
$25.00 • ISBN 0973467126

**Canadian Bestseller and Winner of the 2005 IPPY Award
for Best North American Travel Memoir!**

"Jackson's humor and charm shine throughout his storytelling."
- Canadian Geographic Magazine

I Sold My Gold Tooth
for Gas Money

Edited by Matt Jackson

Traveling is not for the timid of heart. What can go wrong often does, as twenty-six travel-hardened writers relate in this book.

Humor/Travel • Softcover • 216 pages
$19.95 • ISBN 0973467142

About Matt Jackson

A graduate of a Wilfrid Laurier's Business Administration program in Waterloo, Canada, Matt Jackson was lured away from the corporate world by the thrill of adventure journalism while still a university student. He is now an author, editor, photojournalist and professional speaker, and is president of Summit Studios, a publishing company specializing in books about travel and the outdoors.

Matt's first book, *The Canada Chronicles: A Four-year Hitchhiking Odyssey*, is a Canadian bestseller and won the IPPY award for best North American travel memoir in 2004. He has also been featured in more than two dozen popular magazines including *Canadian Geographic, Backpacker, Paddler, Canoe & Kayak* and *BBC Wildlife*.

He currently lives with his wife Stacey in Vancouver, BC, where they spend as much time hiking and kayaking as possible.